Contents

Plot
Chapter 1	4
Chapters 2–4	6
Chapters 5–7	8
Chapters 8–10	10
Chapters 11–13	12
Chapters 14–16	14
Chapters 17–20	16
Chapters 21–24	18
Chapters 25–27	20
Chapters 28–30	22
Chapters 31–34	24
Chapters 35–38	26
Chapters 39–42	28
Narrative Form and Structure	30

Setting and Context
Settings: Carol's Flat, Maureen's House, Sylvia's House and the Allotments	32
Historical Context	34
Literary Context	36

Characters
Leon	38
Carol	40
Maureen	42
Sylvia	44
Tufty Burrows	46
Mr Devlin (Victor)	48

Themes
Isolation and Community	50
Race and Racialised Identity	52
Family and Parenting	54
Childhood	56
Mental Health and Social Services	58

The Exam
Tips and Assessment Objectives	60
Practice Questions	62
Planning a Character Question Response	64
Grade 5 Annotated Response	66
Grade 7+ Annotated Response	68
Planning a Theme Question Response	70
Grade 5 Annotated Response	72
Grade 7+ Annotated Response	74

Glossary 76

Answers 77

Chapter 1

Plot

You must be able to: understand how characters are introduced in the opening chapter.

Who are the first characters to be introduced?

Leon, the **protagonist** of the novel, is presented as being kind and instantly loving towards his new baby brother. His first conversation with his little brother shows his innocence, as he tells him about his favourite TV programme, *The Dukes of Hazzard*, and his school. He also tells him his own date of birth: 5 July 1971. The novel opens in 1980; Leon is nearly nine. He knows the baby will not be able to answer him, but he carries on as if the baby understands. This conversation is a narrative device that tells the reader about Leon.

Carol is Leon's mother. The reader quickly realises that she is white, whereas Leon is of mixed-race heritage as his father was Black. She is attractive to men. Leon tells the baby that 'she's beautiful. Everyone's always saying it.' At this point in the novel, Carol seems very loving towards both her children. Despite having a new baby, she comes 'straight over' to Leon and 'kisses his cheek and his forehead', demonstrating her continued affection and attentiveness towards him.

Tina is Carol's friend and neighbour. She has more traditional views of parenting. Unlike Carol, who lets Leon call her by her given name, she insists on 'Mum' and 'Auntie Tina', creating a **hierarchy** between children and adults.

Jake is Leon's new baby brother, although the reader doesn't learn his name yet.

How is the plot introduced?

Kit de Waal plunges the reader into Leon's world by placing him in a hospital room just after the birth of his new baby brother. The innocence and tenderness that will characterise their relationship throughout the text is soon apparent.

One of the key features of the book is the idea that Leon looks older than his age. The nurse comments: 'you're nice and big for your age. A right little man.' While this may seem to be a compliment, it becomes a running theme of the text – Leon, due to his size, and possibly his race, is frequently mistaken for being older and is treated differently as a result.

We also get an indication of Carol's inconsistency or absence as a parent with the reference to the fact that Tina's boyfriend 'always says, "Again?"' when he sees Leon at Tina's flat, with the adverb 'again' suggesting that Tina often looks after Leon for Carol. Carol also puts off feeding the baby because she is 'just going to the smoking room'. Despite this, she does seem to appreciate her children: 'I've got two beautiful, beautiful boys.'

How to Use Your Snap Revision Text Guide

This *My Name is Leon* Snap Revision Text Guide will help you get a top mark in your AQA English Literature exam. It is divided into two-page topics so that you can easily find help for the bits you find tricky. This book covers everything you will need to know for the exam:

Plot: what happens in the novel?

Setting and Context: what periods, places, events and attitudes are relevant to understanding the novel?

Characters: who are the main characters, how are they presented, and how do they change?

Themes: what ideas does the author explore in the novel, and how are they shown?

The Exam: what kinds of question will come up in your exam, and how can you get top marks?

To help you get ready for your exam, each two-page topic includes the following:

Key Quotations to Learn
Short quotations to memorise that will allow you to analyse in the exam and boost your grade.

Summary
A recap of the most important points covered in the topic.

Sample Analysis
An example of the kind of analysis that the examiner will be looking for.

Quick Test
A quick-fire test to check you can remember the main points from the topic.

Exam Practice
A short writing task so you can practise applying what you've covered in the topic.

Glossary
A handy list of words you will find useful when revising *My Name is Leon* with easy-to-understand definitions.

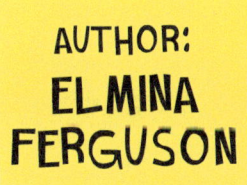

AUTHOR: ELMINA FERGUSON

ebook

To access the ebook version of this Snap Revision Text Guide, visit **collinshub.co.uk/ebooks** and follow the step-by-step instructions.

Published by Collins
An imprint of Harper*Collins*Publishers
1 London Bridge Street
London SE1 9GF

Harper*Collins*Publishers
Macken House, 39/40 Mayor Street Upper,
Dublin 1, D01 C9W8, Ireland

© Harper*Collins*Publishers Limited 2025

ISBN 978-0-00-876892-8

First published 2025

10 9 8 7 6 5 4 3 2

All rights reserved. No part of this publication may be reproduced, stored in a retrieval system, or transmitted, in any form or by any means, electronic, mechanical, photocopying, recording or otherwise, without the prior permission of Collins.

Without limiting the exclusive rights of any author, contributor or the publisher of this publication, any unauthorised use of this publication to train generative artificial intelligence (AI) technologies is expressly prohibited. HarperCollins also exercise their rights under Article 4(3) of the Digital Single Market Directive 2019/790 and expressly reserve this publication from the text and data mining exception.

British Library Cataloguing in Publication Data.

A CIP record of this book is available from the British Library.

Commissioning Editor: Clare Souza
Managing Editor: Shelley Teasdale
Author: Elmina Ferguson
Contributor: Steve Eddy
Typesetting: QBS Learning
Cover designers: Kneath Associates and Sarah Duxbury
Production: Bethany Brohm
Printed in the United Kingdom

ACKNOWLEDGEMENTS

The author and publisher are grateful to the copyright holders for permission to use quoted materials and images.

Every effort has been made to trace copyright holders and obtain their permission for the use of copyright material. The author and publisher will gladly receive information enabling them to rectify any error or omission in subsequent editions. All facts are correct at time of going to press.

My Name Is Leon by Kit de Waal published by Viking. Copyright © Kit de Waal, 2016. Reprinted by permission of Penguin Books Limited.

What indications does the reader get about Leon's life so far?

The reader learns that Leon and his mother live in a flat next to a busy dual carriageway. Tina lives in the flat next door. She has a toddler whom Leon calls Wobbly Bobby, and Leon has to share Bobby's bedroom when he sleeps at Tina's. Leon is kind to Bobby and, as a result, 'Bobby loves Leon.' Leon's familiarity with the flat shows how often he is there.

Key Quotations to Learn

'… you're nice and big for your age. A right little man.'

'I won't drop you,' he says. 'I'm big for my age.'

… he always says, 'Again?' and Tina says, 'I know.'

Summary

- Leon is at the hospital following the birth of his new baby brother.
- He instantly bonds with his brother.
- Leon already adores his brother and wants to protect him and teach him about the world.
- Carol already shows some signs of being absent and emotionally distant.

Questions

QUICK TEST
1. How old is Leon?
2. How do others misjudge Leon, based on his size?
3. What year is the first chapter set in?
4. What is Leon's favourite TV programme?
5. Who does Leon often stay with?

EXAM PRACTICE
Write a paragraph analysing how Leon's character is established in the opening chapter of the novel.

> Plot

Chapters 2–4

You must be able to: understand how Carol treats Leon and his perception of how Jake's father treats her.

How does Leon's character develop in these chapters?

In Chapter 2, Carol is shown taking advantage of Leon's willingness to help out with his brother when she says it is 'too wet and rainy' for him to go to school and leaves him 'in charge' with baby Jake. While De Waal does not focus closely on this, it shows Carol's over-reliance on Leon. He becomes not just a big brother, but almost a parent to Jake.

When Leon sees Carol's boyfriend Tony in Chapter 4, he sees him as a 'bad guy from James Bond'. This implies that Leon regards him as an intruder in his home. Leon plays out a fantasy of defending his mother and himself against him, as if he is in a Western film. This indicates that Leon is perceptive, as Tony does have some villainous character traits. For example, he is cheating on his partner with Carol and he is refusing to take responsibility for Jake, his newborn baby with her. The reader sees how observant Leon is when he notices that the man speaks 'slowly with his head on one side like his mum is a baby or she's a bit slow'. This is exactly what is happening, as Tony is trying to calm Carol down and make her leave him alone.

At the end of Chapter 4, after a new boy at school says he has trained his poodle to bite people, Leon fantasises about training a dog to bite Tony and other people he feels threatened by.

What do we learn about Carol?

Carol is characterised as a fantasist who pretends that everything is going well even when it isn't. Her insistence in Chapter 3 that Tony wants to be with her and wants to 'settle down for good' seems **naïve** and based on wishful thinking. De Waal emphasises this with Tina's questions; for instance, 'What about his daughter?' when Carol is suggesting that they will all move in together.

Chapter 3 begins with 'Leon has begun to notice the things that make his mum cry'. This shows that he is observant and tuned in to his mother and helps the reader realise that Carol's mental health has been declining since Jake's birth. De Waal follows this statement with a list of her financial and emotional stresses. When Tony describes her as 'beautiful' but with a 'brain like a rusty motor' in Chapter 4, the **simile** seems harsh. It suggests that, behind her beauty, she is becoming detached from reality. Tina mentioned in Chapter 2 that 'You still look tired, Cal' and Leon has noticed that his mum keeps crying, but Tony's harsh comment underlines what De Waal is hinting at – that Carol is suffering from post-natal depression. Perhaps this is why Carol makes Leon promise to look after his brother and himself.

Tony's lack of sympathy links to contextual understandings of mental health: in the early 1980s, mental illness was considered a **stigma**. His only concern is to get rid of Carol and to avoid responsibility for the baby. The author makes this clear when his voice goes hard and she 'jerks her head like he's slapped her' and he issues a veiled threat: '… start behaving yourself'.

Key Quotations to Learn

'I'm your brother,' says Leon. 'Big brother.' (Chapter 2)
Leon has begun to notice the things that make his mum cry … (Chapter 3)
'… you've got a brain like a rusty motor.' (Tony, Chapter 4)

Summary

- Carol brings baby Jake home.
- Carol is showing increased signs of low mood.
- Leon looks after the baby a lot.
- Jake's father Tony wants nothing to do with Carol or Jake.

Questions

QUICK TEST
1. What excuse does Carol make to keep Leon off school?
2. What question does Tina ask Carol that hints at Carol not being realistic?
3. What does the fact that Leon notices the things that make Carol cry reveal about him?
4. What does Carol make Leon promise in Chapter 4?
5. Why does Leon want a dog at the end of Chapter 4?

EXAM PRACTICE
Write a paragraph explaining how Carol is presented in Chapters 2–4 of *My Name is Leon*.

Plot — Chapters 5–7

You must be able to: understand how Leon's life changes in these chapters.

What do we learn about Leon's life in these chapters?

Chapter 5 begins in the summer holidays when things are described as being 'jangled' because there is even less structure in Leon's life than usual. Leon has the freedom to go to bed whenever he wants and eat whatever he wants, but 'there's nothing in the fridge and nothing in the cupboard'. This is the first time his stealing is mentioned: he steals coins from Carol's purse.

Leon gets angry at his mother, possibly due to him understanding, on some level, the neglect that he is experiencing. His 'good system' for Jake is heartwarming. In Chapter 5, De Waal includes a lot of detail that shows how thoughtful and intelligent Leon is. However, while the reader does see Leon's capabilities and strength of character, this section is also frightening as his efforts are unsustainable, considering his age. Things come to a head when Carol overdoses and Leon can't wake her up. **Social Services** have to be called in when Carol is taken to hospital.

Information is provided about Leon's father in Chapter 5 when Tina mentions to the **social worker** that he 'wasn't much use' and that he was 'inside for a bit', a slang term for having been in prison. It also becomes apparent from the comment 'The last time things were like this' that Leon previously had to go to a **foster parent**. It is evident that Leon has been desperately trying to protect not just Jake, but also Carol. At the end of Chapter 5, Leon is again taken into care and he and Jake are driven to a foster carer's home.

Chapter 6 gives further information about Carol's 'drug dependency', her 'breakdown' and the children being '**malnourished**' – all revealed through the narrative device of Leon eavesdropping on the foster carer Maureen's conversation with a social worker Leon dubs 'the Zebra'.

Chapter 7 shows that Leon is struggling to sleep, suggesting that he is still reliving the trauma of his parents' relationship. De Waal incorporates several flashbacks of incidents that had interrupted Leon's dreams in the past, such as his father and mother having an argument, to give us more background about Leon's life with his mum.

What do we learn about Carol?

Carol's mental health issues have deteriorated. Leon has been trying to get his mother up for days, demonstrating how serious her condition has become. She and Tina have fallen out because Tina is fed up with Carol taking advantage of her and 'cos she keeps borrowing money'. Carol has distanced herself from her own friendships and is not taking responsibility for her children and her finances.

There is a history of alcohol use in the family, which may also help to explain Carol's difficult family history and her struggle to provide consistent care for Leon, which ultimately leads to a breakdown in caregiving. After the overdose, Tina tells the social worker that 'Both of them drank', meaning Leon's father and Carol.

How is Maureen different from Carol?

In Chapter 6, Leon's new foster mother, Maureen, is introduced. One of the things that characterises Maureen is her desire to feed Leon. The first thing she gives him is a Jammie Dodger biscuit. On his first morning with her, 'The smell of breakfast fills Leon's nose and cramps his belly.' The verb 'cramps' shows the physical pain Leon has endured due to hunger. This section can also be read as a **metaphor** for Leon's emotional hunger. Just as the cupboards in his home have 'nothing', Leon is also emotionally empty. In Maureen's house, there is a giant wooden spoon that says 'Best Mum'. This seems to represent her role as a **nurturer**. This also contrasts with Carol's lack of parental capacity. Maureen is presented as an experienced and confident foster mother with 'an eye for kids'.

Key Quotations to Learn

She goes to bed all the time so Leon has to do everything. (Chapter 5, about Carol)

Jake has been crying all morning and Carol won't do anything. (Chapter 5)

It tastes like the best thing in the world ... (Chapter 6, about the sandwich Maureen gives him)

Summary

- Leon tries to manage the household, but Carol takes an overdose.
- Social Services become involved.
- Jake and Leon are taken into care.
- Maureen, their new foster mother, welcomes them to her home.
- Maureen immediately seems to be a nurturing character.

Questions

QUICK TEST
1. What does Leon take from Carol in Chapter 5?
2. Why have Carol and Tina stopped being friends?
3. What do we learn about the relationship between Carol and Leon's father?
4. What does Maureen immediately give Leon?
5. What does Maureen say she has an eye for?

EXAM PRACTICE
Write a paragraph exploring how De Waal contrasts Carol and Maureen.

| Plot | **Chapters 8–10** |

You must be able to: consider how prejudices are presented in these three chapters.

What do we learn about Leon's character and history during these chapters?

Leon appears to enjoy the constant onslaught of food that Maureen provides: 'It's impossible to choose a favourite dinner at Maureen's house.' Leon had previously been starved, sometimes of food and more often of affection. It is telling that when he gets frustrated because he thinks Maureen is treating him like 'a baby', he says, 'I'm not hungry': he rejects Maureen's affection by rejecting her food. His anger at being treated like a child also hints that he has been **adultified**. However, Chapter 8 ends with a happy moment when he celebrates Christmas with Maureen and Jake and is delighted to receive presents he really wants – including two Action Man dolls.

Maureen's nickname for Leon, 'pigeon', could just imply her affection for him and her sense of his vulnerability. However, pigeons often symbolise loyalty, so this could represent Leon's unwavering loyalty to his mother and to baby Jake.

How do racial issues affect Jake's adoption and Leon's fostering?

In Chapter 9, Maureen says, quite bluntly, that Jake is getting adopted 'Because he's a baby, a white baby. And you're not.' While a lot of the racism in this novel is implicit, these statements show her honesty. Instead of just making an excuse, Maureen bluntly tells Leon the truth. The other adults may be aware that Jake is partly being adopted because of his skin tone, but only Maureen is willing to say this. The fact that Maureen uses the adjective 'white' to emphasise their differences also shows how starkly the world sees them.

Leon describes Jake as 'perfection'. This may convey his unconditional love for his brother, but it also makes the reader wonder whether Jake's perfection is linked to his whiteness. This could indicate that Leon has inherited some slightly racialised views.

How does De Waal create a sense of tension and suspense in Chapter 9?

In Chapter 9, De Waal **foreshadows** a shift that is about to occur. The repetition in 'The air is different' and 'The air has been different since yesterday' creates a sense that a significant change is coming. This is further presented in the phrase 'Someone is coming.' The use of the pronoun 'someone' makes this moment **ominous**. The reader may hope that it is someone who is going to bring positivity into Leon's difficult situation, but they are more aware than Leon that it is more likely to be something challenging.

The conversation between Salma, Jake's social worker, and Leon in Chapter 9 contains a **subtext** that adds tension to their interaction. For instance, Salma's question, 'You love Jake, don't you, Leon?', is subtly **manipulative**. Salma knows that Leon loves Jake, and by getting him to say so, she is building up to suggesting that if he really loves Jake, he would want him to be adopted, even if Leon then loses contact with him. Perhaps she is trying to use Leon's love for Jake to limit his anger or sadness, or even to justify it to herself. There is also a **disparity** of power between Salma and Leon. He may realise that his answers will change nothing. The ominous undertones of the conversation come to fruition in Chapter 10, when a couple come to take Jake away. Chapter 10 is relatively short, adding to the abruptness of this massive change. Leon shows his grief and anger by making a mess of his bedroom.

Key Quotations to Learn

It's impossible to choose a favourite dinner at Maureen's house. (Chapter 8)
'Because he's a baby, a white baby. And you're not.' (Maureen, Chapter 9)
The lady doesn't look at Leon, she only looks at Jake … (Chapter 10)

Summary

- Leon has a pleasant Christmas with Jake and Maureen.
- Leon and Jake are treated differently because Leon is mixed-race and Jake is white.
- Salma tries to convince Leon that Jake's **adoption** is for the best.
- A couple come to adopt Jake.

Questions

QUICK TEST
1. Why does Leon get frustrated with Maureen in Chapter 8?
2. What Christmas presents is Leon especially pleased to get?
3. What reason does Maureen give Leon for Jake being adopted?
4. How does Salma try to prepare Leon for Jake being adopted?
5. How does Leon respond to Jake's adoption?

EXAM PRACTICE
Write a paragraph to explore how De Waal presents the effects of prejudice in these chapters.

Plot

Chapters 11–13

You must be able to: analyse the shifts in Leon's and Carol's characters.

How has Leon's mental health deteriorated?

Chapter 11 opens with Leon being woken from a night terror. Maureen exclaims 'Leon! Leon!' as well as 'You're grinding your teeth again, Leon!' Grinding teeth is often a sign of stress and anxiety; De Waal further conveys this with the description of Leon's nightmare: 'He was fighting an evil monster …' The evil monster could be a metaphor for the threats that Leon faces.

Leon's anxiety is also expressed through anger. For instance, when he vandalises Salma's bag in Chapter 12, it is obvious that he is exerting the only kind of control and **autonomy** that he has. He realises that he can do very little to change the outcomes of his life. However, the 'brown sticky mess' that he creates is his way of harming someone he believes has harmed him.

Maureen sympathises with Leon. When she states that 'You've split them up and in my books that's a sin' (Chapter 12), De Waal is suggesting that Social Services have failed Leon. Her use of the sentence tag 'Maureen snorts', with the explosive sound of 'snorts', helps to highlight Maureen's frustration.

How is Carol's deteriorating mental health portrayed?

In Chapter 12, De Waal uses the device of an **epistolary text**, in this case a letter from Social Services contained in a set of file notes on Jake's case, which interrupts the usual narrative voice. The straightforward and emotionally detached tone of the letter shows the severity of Carol's mental health crisis. It also provides more history, such as the fact that Carol's mother and maternal grandmother both had psychiatric disorders. It seems that Carol may never be able to care for Leon.

The letter includes a list of medical issues that Carol suffers from, including 'anxiety, restlessness, **stupor** and transient mood swings into hypomania'. The list is used to convey the gravity of Carol's mental health problems. Some of the symptoms appear to contradict one another – stupor and restlessness are opposites. This helps to show the complexity of her mental health issues. However, what is most noticeable is the lack of **empathy** in the letter. Its factual tone reminds the reader that Carol is being looked after by professionals who have a duty of care towards her, but who do not know and love her as a person the way that Leon or other friends or family members might. The care they show her is expressed in clinical terms that identify her symptoms but cannot express empathy for her as a person. This reflects the medical attitude towards mental health that existed in the early 1980s. Instead of seeking to fully understand Carol's issues, the professionals merely label her separate symptoms.

How is foreshadowing used in Chapter 13?

Maureen struggling to climb the hill leading to her sister Sylvia's house in Chapter 13 is the first indication that she has health issues, although she tries to downplay it: 'Got a tight chest, that's all.' The possibility of her health collapsing is further foreshadowed by Sylvia pleading with her, 'Promise me, Mo. The doctor.' The repetition of 'Promise me' later in the conversation clearly shows Sylvia's desire for real assurance. Later on, Leon also says 'You have to go to the doctor' with the modal verb 'have' hinting at the gravity of Maureen's failing health.

Key Quotations to Learn

'… I think about you and I care for you and I love you.' (Maureen, Chapter 11)

'You've split them up and in my books that's a sin …' (Maureen, Chapter 12)

'You have to go to the doctor.' (Leon, Chapter 13)

Summary

- Leon has night terrors and grinds his teeth.
- Leon reads a letter from Social Services detailing Carol's problems.
- Carol is too unwell to look after either of her children.
- Leon and Maureen visit Maureen's sister Sylvia.
- It emerges that Maureen hasn't been feeling very well.

Questions

QUICK TEST

1. What does Leon keep doing in his sleep?
2. What does Leon find in Salma's bag?
3. Why can't Carol look after her children?
4. What is the tone of the letter from Social Services?
5. What does Sylvia get Maureen to promise?

EXAM PRACTICE

Write a paragraph exploring how De Waal presents Leon's deteriorating mental health in these chapters.

> Plot

Chapters 14–16

You must be able to: explore the differences between Carol, Maureen and Sylvia.

How is Carol's irresponsibility conveyed to the reader?

In Chapter 14, the reader finally sees Carol again and De Waal clearly presents her immaturity and lack of maternal instinct towards Leon. First, the author uses the familiar narrative device of Leon eavesdropping. He hears Maureen saying 'bad things' about Carol on the phone. She acknowledges that Carol is ill, but is still unimpressed by the way she has treated her children.

When Carol comes to visit Leon, she focuses on having lost Jake rather than on Leon. When she sees Leon's photo of Jake, she collapses and Leon has to fetch Maureen. When she asks if she can have the photo, Leon's only connection to his younger brother, Maureen forcefully refuses. However, Carol's irresponsibility results in him acting more like the parent and he runs after her with the photo. This shows the subversion of their roles. Leon's emotional response is a 'dark star of pain in his throat', which may suggest he is trying to suppress anger or tears.

While Leon is often concerned with Carol's happiness, she does not have the same concern for him. This is indicated by the lacklustre gift she gives him – a pencil and pen set in a wooden box. Compare this with the thoughtfully chosen Christmas presents Maureen gives him in Chapter 8. While Carol does show some affection towards him, she soon seems anxious to leave and get back to her boyfriend Alan.

Leon's perceptions of Carol indicate how much she has changed: 'Her teeth and her fingers are yellowy brown like mustard and her cheeks go in like a skeleton.' This could also be interpreted as De Waal showing that Leon's perception of her as now being unattractive represents his growing awareness of her shortcomings as a parent.

How does Leon respond to Maureen's illness?

The concerns about Maureen's health were raised at the end of Chapter 13. De Waal has used Chapter 14's meeting between Leon and Carol to make the reader forget the other stressful issue in Leon's life. Bringing it back to the reader's attention in Chapter 15 heightens the pathos of the situation, as the reader sees Leon losing two maternal figures in successive chapters. Sylvia calling him 'a proper little man' is symbolic of the painful adultification of his life. He is forced to behave as an adult, due to the stresses of his life. This adds to the pain the reader feels for Leon. Despite his maturity, he does not have the autonomy of an adult.

What is Leon's life like at Sylvia's house?

Chapter 16 opens with a list of the things that Leon dislikes, the first being Sylvia herself, and most of the others relating to her. His life at Sylvia's house is considerably less happy than his life at Maureen's. Rather than the camaraderie he shared with Maureen, there is constant upheaval and change, creating frustration and anger. The reintroduction of the Zebra and her gift of a BMX bike for Leon ends the chapter in a much more positive way. The bike offers Leon a new freedom, and his first bike ride is, perhaps, the first time in the narrative that he is able to follow his own instincts and direction.

Key Quotations to Learn

[Leon] feels a dark star of pain in his throat … (Chapter 14)

… it's like spilling a glass of pop, everything comes out in a rush and he can't stop the tears … (Chapter 15)

There are too many things that Leon doesn't like and he's made a list of them in his head. (Chapter 16)

Summary

- Carol visits Leon.
- Maureen becomes very ill and has to go into hospital.
- Leon has to move in with Sylvia, whom he dislikes.
- The Zebra explains that Leon cannot look after Carol.
- The Zebra gives Leon a BMX bike.

Questions

QUICK TEST
1. What does Carol do when she sees Leon's photo of Jake?
2. What does Maureen not want Carol to have?
3. What gift does Carol give Leon?
4. What comes first in Leon's list of things he dislikes?
5. What gift does the Zebra give Leon?

EXAM PRACTICE
Write a paragraph explaining how De Waal uses Carol and Maureen as **dramatic foils** to each other in these chapters.

Plot

Chapters 17–20

You must be able to: understand how De Waal uses context to support the narrative.

How do the allotments represent growth?

The introduction of Tufty, a young Black man whom Leon becomes increasingly close to, is significant as this is the first male character (apart from Jake) that Leon feels close to. Tufty's nickname for Leon, 'Star', shows a connection and a warmth that Leon has not experienced since Maureen's illness. This warmth is also shown when he gives Leon a cream soda (Chapter 17).

A key focus is Tufty teaching Leon how to garden in his **allotment.** This is described in Chapter 18 and can be seen as a metaphor for their relationship – Tufty encourages Leon to grow. As the first Black character in the text (Leon's father is only mentioned in flashbacks), Tufty gives Leon a deeper introduction to the culture and history of the racial identity he inherited from his father, an identity that is a source of joy, pride and empowerment for Tufty and which he seems keen to share with Leon. The images of Black men in Tufty's shed are an important message about the power of role models.

Tufty is described as having 'a wide smile and big teeth' and his kindness towards Leon is a key part of Leon's emotional growth. He can be contrasted with Leon's absent father. In Chapter 20, Tufty describes some shooting seeds as '… babies. Fragile. Babies need looking after.' While this is about the nurturing that seeds need, it also relates to Leon's needs.

Also at the allotments, Leon meets Mr Devlin, who teaches Leon about his Japanese knife.

How are multiculturalism and racial tension presented?

One of the key shifts of life at Sylvia's home is that the area near her house has far more Black people than Leon's previous home. The references in Chapter 17 to 'Pakistani shops', 'funny-looking vegetables', 'old Indian men in turbans' and 'Black women in bright African headdresses' suggest that Leon is not used to living in a culturally diverse area. Together with Tufty's introduction to Black music and history, Leon's world is expanding as he faces new challenges. It is mentioned that 'No one notices Leon.' This can be seen as positive, in that he now blends in due to the diversity of those around him.

Despite this representation of **multiculturalism,** Chapter 20 hints at the racialised violence that Black people were subjected to during the early 1980s when a minor Black character, Castro, asks: 'You don't see what the police is doing to black people?' As the author keeps mentioning that Leon looks older than his age, and he now thinks he could look 14, the reader may worry about how his appearance as a young Black male will impact his treatment by others.

By presenting the differences between Mr Johnson, an older Black man, Tufty, with his exuberance and warmth, and Castro, with his justified anger towards racism, De Waal ensures that the novel presents a varied view of Black men, composed of different generations and different attitudes.

What do we learn in Chapter 19?

In Chapter 19, Leon finally gets to visit Maureen in the hospital. This serves as a reminder of their closeness. Describing Maureen 'with a white tube in her nose' tells the reader that she is still very unwell. De Waal also uses this chapter to reveal several things the reader would otherwise not know. For instance, Leon has not seen his mother again, he still has no contact with Jake and he's having trouble sleeping. This hints at his mental state but also allows us to understand that Carol's inability to care for Leon remains a painful constant in his life.

Key Quotations to Learn

There are loads more black people than where Sylvia lives … (Chapter 17)

'You still turning the other cheek, eh, Johnson?' (Chapter 20)

'You don't see what the police is doing to black people?' (Castro, Chapter 20)

Summary

- Leon meets Tufty, a young Black man who spends a lot of time on his allotment.
- Tufty begins teaching Leon about gardening.
- Mr Devlin, an Irishman who also has an allotment, teaches Leon about his Japanese knife.
- The Zebra takes Leon to see Maureen in hospital.
- Castro talks about experiences of police brutality.

Questions

QUICK TEST
1. What is Tufty's nickname for Leon?
2. What does Tufty give to Leon?
3. Who takes Leon to see Maureen?
4. What does Mr Devlin show Leon?
5. What is Castro angry about?

EXAM PRACTICE
Write a paragraph explaining Tufty's significance as a character.

> Plot

Chapters 21–24

You must be able to: analyse and discuss how De Waal presents racial tensions.

How does Leon adapt to his new life?

As mentioned in Chapter 16, Leon dislikes his new school. His perception that 'Teachers are like social workers, with lots of different pretend voices and smiles' shows his growing mistrust of adults. He seems to be struggling with the constant turmoil of his home life. Chapter 21 ends with Leon wishing he had a remote control to turn off all the people he does not like – Sylvia, teachers and social workers. The forceful image of him crushing the remote control 'with a big hammer so they could never come on again' shows his anger at his situation.

Another symptom of Leon's sense of deprivation and powerlessness is his continued stealing. When he steals from Sylvia's purse, it seem that he is becoming more devious: 'He leaves lots of other coins in the purse so she won't notice' (Chapter 22). The Zebra comments on how his behaviour 'has got a bit out of hand recently' (Chapter 24).

How are historical events portrayed in these chapters?

Chapter 22 introduces Sylvia's fascination with the Royal Wedding of 1981 between (then) Prince Charles and Lady Diana Spencer. Also introduced is the emerging civil unrest of the period. While not explicitly stated, these are the April 1981 Brixton Riots, a catalyst for riots in cities across the UK. Each was caused by police mistreatment of young Black men and the introduction of stop-and-search procedures which allowed police to search anyone without evidence. This was used to harass people living as minorities in the UK, particularly Black men. At the same time, Bobby Sands, a member of the Irish Republican Army militant group, died in prison as the result of a hunger strike against restrictions placed on him and his comrades by prison authorities. These events put the conflicts faced by Leon into a wider context – his chaotic life and lack of a clear place in society mimic the wider upheaval caused by social injustice and division.

How do we see Tufty's growing influence on Leon?

Chapter 23 has Leon being introduced to a range of musical artists by Tufty. These artists all play reggae or dub music (genres developed and popularised by Black people). It is also interesting to note that, earlier in the chapter, Leon styles himself in a similar way to Tufty, cutting his jeans to make 'his Tufty shorts', representing Tufty's influence on him.

How has Carol's health continued to deteriorate?

Chapter 24 sees the reintroduction of Carol as Leon visits her in the Family Centre. Carol is thinner, looks depressed and is 'holding a little doll and turning it round and round', indicating her descent into an **infantilised** mindset. Leon and Carol's shared pain at losing

Jake is also very apparent. When Leon starts to impersonate Jake, saying 'Yeeeyyii, yeeeyyii, tatta, tatta', we see him descending into a world of make-believe as a means of escaping the painful truth. His hope that he 'could be him [Jake]' as a means of Carol coming back to him is used to end the chapter. While the adults around him, in particular Carol, ignore his needs, he would do anything to mould himself into whatever pleases her.

Key Quotations to Learn

If Leon had a remote control he would lie in bed and turn Sylvia off … (Chapter 21)
She's holding a little doll and turning it round and round … (Chapter 24)
'You could come back for me and, sometimes, I could be him.' (Chapter 24)

Summary

- Leon faces challenges at his new school.
- Plans are being made for a community celebration of the Royal Wedding of Diana and Charles.
- Leon gets to know Mr Devlin more.
- Leon hears Black music on Tufty's new 'boombox'.
- It becomes apparent that there is increasing civil unrest in the neighbourhood.
- Carol's inadequacies as a mother and her mental health challenges continue to be portrayed.

Questions

QUICK TEST
1. What does Leon want to do with his imaginary remote control?
2. Who introduces Leon to Black music?
3. Who comments that Leon's behaviour has got 'a bit out of hand'?
4. How has Carol changed since Leon last saw her?
5. Who does Leon say he could be for Carol?

EXAM PRACTICE
Write a paragraph explaining how De Waal uses historical events to provide context to Leon's experiences.

| Plot | # Chapters 25–27 |

You must be able to: explore how De Waal heightens tension in these chapters.

How are Leon's growing anxieties shown?

Chapter 25 begins with Leon having a nightmare in which he is in a cooking pot and about to be eaten by an ogre. He feels that if he doesn't keep running, a giant's foot will come out of the sky to 'squish him flat'. This could portray Leon's growing anxieties, related to his displacement from his previous homes. He is still at Sylvia's house; Maureen is still unwell; his mother is still unable to look after him. It could also represent the difficulties he faces at school and with social workers or even his growing discomfort of being a young, mixed-race boy in a hostile world. Leon's issues with sleep could link to his lack of power over his life. Being about to be consumed in the dream could represent how every aspect of his identity has been threatened by things beyond his control.

Despite Leon's anxieties, these chapters do show something more positive: his bonding with Sylvia. She looks after him when he is ill and she tells him funny stories about a rabbit. They both find the second one so funny that they lie on the bed together 'rolling from side to side' (Chapter 27).

How is the mystery of Mr Devlin developed?

Mr Devlin, unlike Tufty, seems to be rather guarded. However, these chapters begin to provide an insight into his life. When Leon becomes unwell at the allotment in Chapter 26, Mr Devlin takes him to his shed and the reader sees a gentler side to him. When Leon wakes up, he sees a series of pictures of 'different brown boys', 'lots of knives' and 'a real pistol'. All of these, while not giving a clear understanding of Mr Devlin's life, suggest that he could be a more complex character than previously imagined. The contents of his shed encourage the reader's intrigue about him – what is his relationship with the boys in the pictures? Are the knives and pistol a symbol of violence in Mr Devlin's life?

How is police brutality finally shown, rather than just being hinted at?

Chapter 27 describes an explosive example of police brutality during which Castro and Tufty are questioned and Castro is beaten by the police. At first Leon thinks the police have come to arrest him. There is a vivid **juxtaposition** between Tufty shouting 'Leave him! Leave him! He can't breathe!' as the police drag and assault Castro while, in contrast, DC Green is 'smiling all the time'. Although the novel was written in 2016, this passage evokes the events in the US in 2020 when George Floyd died as a result of being suffocated by a police officer, leading to the 2020 Black Lives Matter protests.

One of Tufty's posters of Black heroes could show Martin Luther King, whose peaceful protests Tufty seems to admire. However, there is also an undercurrent of irritation, as Tufty questions the effectiveness of peaceful protest.

This chapter also clearly presents the police's blatant racism when DC Green says, 'You're all the same with your big mouths and your big lips'. The racism in this phrase is startling – 'big lips' are an often-**caricatured** facial feature in racist imagery of Black people.

Key Quotations to Learn

In Leon's dream he's standing in a cooking pot with white flames licking up the sides. (Chapter 25)

Spit comes out of Castro's mouth like he's a wild dog. (Chapter 27)

'Leave him! Leave him! He can't breathe!' (Chapter 27)

Summary

- Leon becomes more anxious and unwell: he has flu.
- Mr Devlin takes care of Leon when he becomes unwell at the allotment and Leon starts to learn a little more about him while looking around his shed.
- The increasing social unrest becomes apparent when Castro and Tufty are involved in an incident of police brutality at the allotments.
- Leon bonds more with Sylvia when she tells him two funny stories.

Questions

QUICK TEST
1. How does Sylvia begin to bond with Leon?
2. Who has pictures of 'different brown boys' on the wall?
3. How do we see a change in Mr Devlin?
4. Who are the police looking for?
5. What does Leon initially believe the police have come to do?

EXAM PRACTICE
Write a paragraph exploring how De Waal uses symbolism to convey Leon's thoughts and experiences.

Plot

Chapters 28–30

You must be able to: analyse how De Waal presents the complexities of Leon's character.

How does Leon respond to social workers?

Whenever a new social worker is introduced, the reader feels Leon's anger. For instance, when he accuses the new social worker Mike (Earring) of making Jake forget him, 'Leon knows every word that he's going to say' (Chapter 28). This social worker is just another example of the system's failure to give Leon any real stability. When Leon says he wants to go home, he means to Maureen's house, suggesting how nurturing and stabilising her presence was. De Waal introduces so many different social workers that the reader, like Leon, is bombarded with transient characters, sharing in Leon's experience. As a result of Earring's visit, Leon angrily makes a mess of Sylvia's bathroom.

How is more revealed about Mr Devlin and Tufty?

In Chapter 29, Leon learns more about gardening from Mr Devlin, and about weightlifting. However, Tufty arrives, furious because he is being evicted from his allotment. He blames Mr Devlin, calling him a racist, and implies that he is a paedophile because of the pictures on his wall and his interest in Leon. They have a violent argument.

For Leon's birthday, Mr Devlin gives him an allotment – his own 'small patch of the planet'. This moment is heartwarming as Leon is finally able to find some sense of ownership and autonomy.

How are things changing for Leon?

In Chapter 29, Leon's fascination with Mr Devlin's gun leads him to steal it. An aspect of Leon's character is the **dichotomy** between his innocent mindset and his mature understanding. De Waal constantly reminds the reader that Leon is almost at war with himself; this also links to him being frequently described as a 'soldier'. This word is used to convey his resilience; however, at this moment, De Waal seems to be focusing on Leon's innocence. His stealing the gun is, structurally, a significant moment.

De Waal reminds us in Chapter 30 that Leon is only ten years old and that his treatment, and his relative maturity, defy his chronological age. His excitement about his birthday reminds the reader that he is a child. A key moment of his birthday is a 'letter from Jake'. However, the letter does little to alleviate Leon's pain. Both Leon and the reader are aware that Jake's letter is the work of his adoptive parents, making this moment anticlimactic. The separation between Jake and Leon becomes even more pronounced. Leon's birthday is celebrated only with adults, emphasising his isolation: he has no friends his own age.

How does Sylvia's humanity become more evident?

Sylvia may not possess Maureen's maternal instincts, but her care for Leon becomes more prominent in these chapters. For instance, it is revealed that she and Maureen were able to get the social workers to obtain a photo and the 'letter' from Jake. It is also Sylvia who informs the reader that there has been 'Not one single word from his mother' on Leon's birthday. At one point, Sylvia also says, 'We get on. I like you and you like me.' While the reader is aware that Leon does not actually like Sylvia very much, it becomes obvious that Sylvia does have an emotional connection with Leon. This is especially apparent at the end of Chapter 30, when she tells him a long and rather darkly humorous joke about a pig with a wooden leg.

Key Quotations to Learn

It could kill Earring if Leon picked it up and stabbed him through the soft bit of his eye. (Chapter 28)

'We get on. I like you and you like me.' (Sylvia, Chapter 28)

'What you doing with that boy in there?' (Tufty, Chapter 29)

Summary

- Another social worker, Earring, becomes involved with Leon's case.
- Leon angrily makes a mess of the bathroom.
- Tufty has been told he is being evicted from the allotment and blames Mr Devlin. They argue.
- On his tenth birthday, Leon gets presents from Maureen and Sylvia as well as his own allotment.
- Sylvia tells Leon darkly humorous stories.
- Leon steals Mr Devlin's gun.

Questions

QUICK TEST
1. Which social worker does Leon get angry with?
2. Who does Tufty blame for his allotment being taken away?
3. Why is Leon not pleased with the letter he receives?
4. What does Leon take from Mr Devlin?
5. Who does Leon not hear from on his birthday?

EXAM PRACTICE
Write a paragraph exploring how the theme of growing up is presented in these chapters.

Plot

Chapters 31–34

You must be able to: explore how Leon's important relationships develop in these chapters.

What do we learn about Mr Devlin's past?

For the last few chapters, there has been a lot of mystery surrounding the character of Mr Devlin, with his gun, his pictures of boys and his knives. The reader may share Tufty's fears when he asks Leon, 'He touch you?' There have been hints that he has an inappropriate interest in young boys, including Leon. In Chapter 31, however, when Mr Devlin is drunk, it begins to seem that he may in fact not be a bad man. It emerges that he has lost his own son and that he had worked at a school in Brazil.

How does Leon plan to escape?

Leon desperately wants to reunite with Jake and is planning to escape so that he can achieve this. He steals baby food from a supermarket and also considers what else Jake would need, again showing his devotion to his baby brother. Chapter 31 also employs the use of narrative flashbacks to give insights into Leon's past, as well as his family. They mention his paternal grandmother, who died of diabetes. While this is a fleeting moment, it helps us to understand Leon's ethnic background. Interestingly, most of his family, both biological and foster, have been white. However, his Black grandmother may have helped Leon to understand his cultural heritage.

How do the police treat Castro?

In Chapter 27, Castro was dragged out of the allotment by the police: a clear image of police brutality. In Chapter 31, he is described with 'blood on his lips' and one of his eyes 'swollen and closed', revealing the full picture of police violence. Leon finds Castro hiding in Tufty's shed. Castro is badly hurt and once again Leon finds himself tending to an adult. However, he does this reluctantly. Castro threatens him to prevent him from revealing his whereabouts and makes him steal Mr Devlin's whiskey for him. Leon fantasises about how he could defend himself from Castro. He escapes and runs into Tufty, who protects him.

How does Leon and Tufty's relationship develop?

It becomes increasingly clear that Leon sees Tufty as a father figure. It's even stated in Chapter 33 that 'Sometimes, when Tufty is talking, Leon thinks about his dad'. However, rather than the immature and volatile behaviour that characterises Leon's father, Tufty is largely characterised by kindness and gentleness. Another key aspect of Tufty's influence is his poetry. His poem 'Ode to Castro' is a blistering critique of police brutality. A key feature of his poetry is the use of the collective pronoun 'we'. This is possibly what makes Leon feel so loved and excited – the inclusion, as well as Tufty's absolute pride in his culture.

How is Maureen now?

Chapter 34 begins with the news that Maureen is going to be discharged. This means Leon 'will go back to his second bedroom'. Again, the reader is reminded that he feels a sense of belonging with Maureen. When Sylvia drunkenly says that 'We're going to move to the seaside … Me and Mo', the reader instantly worries that Leon will once again be placed in a new environment, one that takes him even further from home, or even that he will be left behind. The chapter ends with Leon once more taking care of an adult. He tells drunken Sylvia, 'Don't cry … Maureen is coming home tomorrow.'

Key Quotations to Learn

'I was loved. They loved me.' (Mr Devlin, Chapter 31)

Sylvia and Leon both think of the rabbit story and smile at each other. (Chapter 32)

'We are the consequences of history / We are the warriors you made.' (Tufty's poem, Chapter 33)

Summary

- More is revealed about Mr Devlin's past: he worked in a school in Brazil and had a son.
- Leon makes a plan to escape and reunite with Jake.
- A flashback provides a glimpse of Leon's father and grandmother.
- Castro is on the run from the police: Leon finds him in Tufty's shed.
- Maureen is expected to leave the hospital soon.
- Leon comforts Sylvia after she has a disappointing night out.

Questions

QUICK TEST
1. Where did Mr Devlin used to live?
2. Who has been hiding in Tufty's shed?
3. What does Leon steal from the supermarket?
4. What is Tufty's poem called?
5. Where does Sylvia want to move with Maureen?

EXAM PRACTICE
Write a paragraph exploring how Tufty is presented as a father figure.

Plot

Chapters 35–38

You must be able to: explore how De Waal creates a heightened sense of emotion in these chapters.

What is Leon's plan to reunite with Jake?

In a novel with many changes, one aspect that remains the same is Leon's love for and desire to protect his younger brother Jake. The beginning of Chapter 35 reminds us of the detailed plan that Leon has been concocting to go to Bristol to find Jake. The list of objects that he has, including food, money, the gun and other stolen items, shows us the extent of his plan. It is interesting that De Waal does not give more significance to any single item; for instance, the gun is simply mentioned in the list of all of his belongings. This once again reaffirms Leon's innocence. He has no idea how dangerous the gun could be, nor does he have an understanding of how far away Bristol is. Nonetheless, he is determined.

How does Leon's life change again when Maureen returns?

Chapter 35 reintroduces Maureen. Her proclamation of 'Here he is!' once again shows us her love and enthusiasm for Leon. However, we are continuously reminded of Maureen's health issues, as well as Sylvia's desire to move away with Maureen to the seaside. Both of these exclude Leon and, once again, it seems that he might be placed in a new household. De Waal also juxtaposes Maureen's maternal nature with Sylvia's more detached approach. Maureen is aware that 'He's gone a bit quiet', whereas Sylvia says, 'Look at the size of him. He can take care of himself.'

How is Castro's killing presented?

In previous chapters, Castro has been a victim of police brutality. In Chapter 36, we find out from Tufty that the police have killed him – 'kicked him to death'. It feels like a very clear choice by De Waal not to show Castro's murder, but rather to have Tufty report it. It almost replicates the Chorus in ancient Greek tragedy, who would narrate to the audience the violent events happening offstage. Tufty's recollection is still emotionally heart-wrenching. He says that they 'Killed him'. The straightforward, uncompromising language conveys the brutality of the violence that Castro has had to endure.

This is then contrasted with the riots that break out in protest, as well as the public's perception of the rioters. For instance, Mr Devlin calls them 'savages', conveying the racial prejudice that the protesters would have received. However, De Waal does not demonise Mr Devlin. Rather, she conveys his somewhat ignorant mindset. This is later shown when he calls out for Leon using the word 'Boy', because neither he nor Tufty know his name. Tufty's discomfort comes as a result of the historical relevance of the term 'boy', often used in a derogatory sense towards Black men. However, for Mr Devlin, this is just a term that he was used to using, working in a school in Brazil.

How does Leon get involved in the riots?

Leon, in a desperate bid to be reunited with Jake, finds himself in the middle of the anti-police riots. Chapter 38 ends with Tufty's voice, 'Yo Star!', which interrupts the realisation from the police and those in the riot that Leon has a gun. As mentioned before, there has been a lot of comment that Leon looks large for his age. This, as well as the adultification of Black and mixed-race children, makes us fear the police's retaliation towards Leon.

Key Quotations to Learn

'Look at the size of him. He can take care of himself.' (Sylvia, Chapter 35)

'You think it's funny that the police kill black people?' (Tufty, Chapter 36)

She grabs Leon and squeezes him hard and he squeezes her back. (Chapter 35)

No one is listening. No one ever listens. (Chapter 38)

Summary

- Leon prepares to make an escape to find Jake.
- Castro is killed by the police.
- Maureen is released from the hospital and returns to Leon and Sylvia.
- Leon becomes involved in the riots.

Questions

QUICK TEST
1. What technique does De Waal use that is like ancient Greek tragedy?
2. Why has Leon packed away food, money and Mr Devlin's gun?
3. What does Mr Devlin call the rioters?
4. What has happened to Castro?
5. Where does Leon want to go?

EXAM PRACTICE
Write a paragraph explaining how De Waal increases tension throughout these chapters.

Plot

Chapters 39–42

You must be able to: analyse how De Waal brings the text to a satisfying conclusion.

How does Leon confront the police?

At the start of Chapter 39, Leon, with the gun in his hand, comes face to face with the police. Mr Devlin shouts out that the gun is only wooden. However, the image of Leon confronting the police with a gun is still terrifying. This is then undercut with the crowd injuring Mr Devlin because they mistake him for a police officer, and the policeman brutally beating Tufty. However, what is most provocative is the policeman's racist language towards Leon. For instance, a policeman 'screams' at Leon, 'You little black bastard!' He also assumes that Tufty is his father. However, Leon replies with some of Tufty's poetry, stating: 'We have dignity and worth.' Perhaps De Waal is showing us the power of words and language, especially in the face of violence. The image of the truncheon becomes a symbol of violence, rather than protection. When Leon hands the policeman his helmet and asks him for help – showing surprising kindness and trust, in the circumstances – the policeman responds with profanities. Fortunately, Tufty manages to get Leon and the injured Mr Devlin away from the riot and they make their way to Sylvia's house where she and Maureen take care of them.

What happens at Leon's last meeting with Carol?

In Chapter 41, Maureen ensures that Leon gets to see Carol. In this moment, Carol admits: 'I can't look after you properly, you know that, don't you?' This is, by far, the most honest and clear comment from Carol so far. It also gives a sense of closure to his relationship with his mother. Carol has finally been able to articulate what the reader has understood from the beginning of the novel. Maureen responds by reassuring Leon that he will live with her and Sylvia from now on.

How does the novel end happily?

The final chapter of the novel takes place on the day of the royal wedding between (then) Prince Charles and the late Princess Diana. Even Mr Devlin, who as an Irishman does not identify with the British Royal Family, is able to enjoy the event as a communal celebration. Leon is surrounded by what has become his new family: Sylvia, Maureen, Mr Devlin (who now seems to be in a romantic relationship with Sylvia) and Tufty. The final image is one of hope, as Leon, despite not having biological family around him, is surrounded by individuals who love him. In Tufty, he has a paternal figure who connects him to his Caribbean heritage. Leon has also become a surrogate son to Mr Devlin, perhaps helping him come to terms with the loss of his own son. Sylvia and Maureen are two maternal figures who, while imperfect, still love and look after Leon.

Key Quotations to Learn

'You little black bastard!' (Policeman, Chapter 39)

'Civil war, it is' (Maureen, Chapter 40)

'I can't look after you properly …' (Carol, Chapter 41)

'She is not my queen, he is not my prince. I don't believe in royal anything.' (Mr Devlin, Chapter 42)

Summary

- Leon produces a wooden gun at the riot.
- A police officer refuses to help him.
- Tufty gets Leon away to safety.
- Leon sees his mother Carol, and she says she cannot look after him.
- Maureen assures Leon that he will live with her and Sylva for the foreseeable future.
- There is a party to celebrate the Royal Wedding.

Questions

QUICK TEST
1. Who reveals that the gun is wooden?
2. Who gets Leon away from the riot?
3. How does Maureen reassure Leon?
4. What event is happening in the final chapter?
5. Who is Sylvia in a romantic relationship with at the end of the novel?

EXAM PRACTICE
'The ending of the novel is very positive. Leon finally has a family.' Write a paragraph explaining whether you agree with this statement.

| Plot | # Narrative Form and Structure |

You must be able to: identify and analyse De Waal's use of structural and narrative devices.

What is the narrative viewpoint?

De Waal uses a **third-person limited** narrative technique. Although the story is told in the third person, not the first person, it is always from Leon's perspective. This means that we can only have insights into other characters through Leon. This only works because he is very observant, and also quite nosy. The reader frequently learns what other characters are thinking from Leon eavesdropping on their conversations. For example, at the start of Chapter 14, he overhears Maureen on the phone being critical of Carol: 'I'd have to be pretty sick to keep me from my kids, know what I mean?'

Even given the limitations of this narrative style, De Waal is able to choose the characters the novel really focuses on and what aspects of their lives are revealed. Carol, for example, is kept at a distance, which gives her an element of mystery. With Maureen, Sylvia, Tufty and Mr Devlin, the reader never learns their thoughts directly, but can infer them from what they say and do, as narrated from Leon's perspective.

Another device used to reveal information that Leon could not possibly know is when he tips out the social worker's bag and reads a letter assessing the mental health of his mother. It includes information that he cannot really understand, including that she suffers from 'anxiety, restlessness, stupor and transient mood swings into hypomania'. This narrative device depends on the reader believing that Leon would read the whole letter and not get bored after the first sentence!

What characterises the narrative perspective?

While the text does not mimic the voice of a child, it does convey the innocence and limited understanding of a child. It avoids using sophisticated language that would make the reader more aware of an author behind the child's perspective. The reader often sees Leon's fantasies, such as how he will defend himself from Jake's father or from Castro. Poignantly, Leon also reveals his simple incomprehension of the emotional complications of the adult world – for example, when he cannot understand why his mother could never come to live with him and Maureen.

De Waal uses this innocence at times to keep the reader in suspense, as when she allows the reader to suspect, like Tufty does, that Mr Devlin is a paedophile. The truth only emerges near the end of the novel – that he has lost a child and worked in a school in Brazil.

How does De Waal use dramatic irony?

This limited narrative voice also creates an element of **dramatic irony**. There are several instances of things that Leon doesn't understand due to his youth and innocence, but which the reader will probably understand. For instance, Chapter 3 begins with 'Leon has begun to notice the things that make his mum cry'. This instantly indicates to the reader that Carol's mental health is beginning to suffer. While Leon possibly realises this too, he does not understand the danger he could be in as a result.

Another key moment occurs in Chapter 38, which could be interpreted as the dramatic climax of the text. Leon finds himself in the midst of a protest turned riot due to police brutality. While others shout and chant 'Justice! Justice! Justice!', Leon shouts 'Dovedale Road!', not realising the peril he is in.

Key Quotations to Learn

Leon has begun to notice the things that make his mum cry ... (Chapter 3)

He can tell when Maureen's trying to be happy and when she's worried ... (Chapter 13)

Maureen has had her no-nonsense voice on all day. (Chapter 14)

There are too many things that Leon doesn't like and he's made a list of them in his head. (Chapter 16)

Summary

- De Waal uses a third-person limited narrative viewpoint.
- Information about other characters can only be revealed through what Leon hears, observes or reads.
- The language of the narrative is believably unsophisticated, but it does not attempt to sound exactly like that of a child.
- Leon's narrative voice often shows a childlike innocence.

Questions

QUICK TEST
1. What perspective does the novel adopt?
2. How is information revealed through a letter at one point?
3. Why is it important to the narrative that Leon often eavesdrops?
4. Which character remains a mystery until near the end of the novel?

EXAM PRACTICE
De Waal's use of narrative style builds empathy for Leon. Using one or more of the 'Key quotations to learn', explain to what extent you agree.

> **Setting and Context**

Settings: Carol's Flat, Maureen's House, Sylvia's House and the Allotments

You must be able to: explain the importance of the different settings in the novel.

In what city is the novel mainly set?

My Name is Leon is predominantly set in Birmingham in 1981. Birmingham is Britain's second largest city after London and is now, and was then, made up of a diverse set of communities. A key setting within Birmingham is Handsworth, known for its multicultural population and its large Black community. In 1981, Handsworth was the scene of civil unrest. It had often been portrayed as a symbol of multicultural unity. However, Black youth in the area frequently disputed this claim and spoke of unfair treatment by the police. In particular, in 1981, the wrongful imprisonment of a young Black man caused anger and dissidence. This was also exacerbated by the riots in other cities, particularly in Brixton, London.

What is Carol's flat like?

Carol's flat is presented as chaotic. In Chapter 5, one of the key aspects is that there is nothing in the fridge. Also, her flat is incredibly untidy. This is juxtaposed with the order and cleanliness of her neighbour Tina's flat, which 'always has a window open and smells of baby lotion'. Carol's flat is used to show the chaos that Leon is being brought up in. In fact, Leon's embarrassment that he should have tidied up before letting Tina in shows that the roles of mother and son have been inverted.

What is Maureen's house like?

Conversely, the first description we get of Maureen's house is of the 'soft, warm bed' that she puts Leon in. 'Soft' and 'warm' are also adjectives that describe Maureen's personality. A key feature of Maureen's home is the amount of food that she gives Leon. For instance, Chapter 8 opens with 'It's impossible to choose a favourite dinner at Maureen's house.' While Leon is emotionally and physically starved at Carol's house, at Maureen's house, he is constantly fed.

What is Sylvia's house like?

Sylvia's house represents her: somewhat **idiosyncratic** and inflexible. For instance, the 'pink sheets' are obviously for her, rather than the football sheets that Maureen gives to Leon. In Sylvia's house, Leon feels like he's an unwanted guest.

De Waal uses different types of imagery across all three main domestic settings. At Carol's flat, everything is about tactile imagery — what Leon can touch and feel. At Maureen's, the imagery is about food, eating and taste. Finally, at Sylvia's house, olfactory imagery, regarding smell, and his dislike and discomfort with Sylvia, is used.

Why are the allotments important?

The allotments are presented as a place where men like Tufty and Mr Devlin can find peace and some personal space. In the novel, they are largely seen as a male space, in contrast to the homes of Maureen and Sylvia. They also become a place where Leon can learn from the two men. In addition, horticultural (plant) imagery is used by De Waal to represent Leon's growth and his burgeoning understanding of the world. It is also used, through the somewhat paternal relationship between Leon and Tufty, as a way to convey Tufty's nurturing of Leon. Through Tufty, Leon seems to almost come to terms with his racial identity, while also finding a satisfying activity in growing vegetables.

Key Quotations to Learn

… there's nothing in the fridge and nothing in the cupboard … (Chapter 5, Carol's house)

Leon is in a soft, warm bed and there are black-and-white footballs on his quilt. (Chapter 6, Maureen's house)

The sheets on his new bed in Sylvia's house. They're pink. (Chapter 16, Sylvia's house)

Summary

- The novel is set largely in Handsworth, Birmingham, in 1981.
- The allotments are a space where Leon learns from Tufty and Mr Devlin.
- Carol's flat is messy and provides little for Leon.
- Maureen's house is nurturing.
- In Sylvia's house, Leon feels like an unwanted guest.

Questions

QUICK TEST
1. Where is the novel largely set?
2. In what year is the novel set?
3. What characterises Carol's home?
4. What kind of imagery does De Waal use with Maureen's home?
5. What is the significance of the allotments?

EXAM PRACTICE
Using one or more of the 'Key quotations to learn', write a paragraph exploring how De Waal uses setting to present Leon's emotional state.

Settings: Carol's Flat, Maureen's House, Sylvia's House and the Allotments

Setting and Context

Historical Context

You must be able to: use the social and historical context to understand the themes and events of the novel.

How does the author's background influence the novel?

Kit de Waal was born in 1960 in Birmingham, the city where *My Name is Leon* is set. She is of mixed-race ancestry, with her father being from St Kitts (an island in the Caribbean) and her mother being of white Irish heritage (like Mr Devlin). This could have influenced her choice of a mixed-race identity for Leon. Furthermore, De Waal's mother, Sheila, was a foster carer and auxiliary nurse. Therefore, De Waal has a deep understanding of the foster care system, having grown up in a household which was involved in it. De Waal herself also worked with the foster care system as an adult. In fact, in an interview with *The Guardian* in 2020, she stated, 'I just wanted to write about a care system that didn't care very much.' De Waal clearly used her personal experience, both as a child growing up and as an adult, to create a very realistic character and situation.

What is the political and social context of the book?

Margaret Thatcher was prime minister of the United Kingdom from 1979 to 1990; *My Name is Leon* is therefore set at the beginning of her time in office. The events for which she is now best known – her sweeping economic reforms, the assassination attempt upon her and her confrontation with the miners' union – lay in the future.

A key event in the novel is the rioting which started in Brixton, South London, and moved to other cities, including the Handsworth area of Birmingham. On 10 April 1981, a protest began due to frustration at stop-and-search laws which allowed the police to stop and search people they suspected of crimes on minimal evidence. This power was widely used to harass people living as minorities in the UK. The riots continued for three days and an estimated 300 people were injured. After the riots, an investigation was carried out by Lord Scarman. He found that there was racial disadvantage, but he denied that institutional racism was present in the police force. However, incidents of police brutality, particularly towards Black males, have long been an issue. We can link this to the murder of Stephen Lawrence in 1993, another key case which exposed the severity of racism and the indifference of the police.

How is the Royal Wedding presented in the book?

The Royal Wedding of Charles and Diana took place in 1981 and was watched by 750 million people worldwide. A momentous occasion which was marked by a public holiday, it was described as a fairy-tale wedding and the wedding of the century. Many people held street parties like the one Sylvia gets so excited about in *My Name is Leon*. The wedding was extremely elaborate and expensive, costing around £81 million in today's money.

Although we now know that there were significant tensions between Charles and Diana, which would eventually lead to their much publicised divorce, at the time, it was seen by many as a celebration of all that was best about Britain.

Key Quotations to Learn

When Lady Diana comes on, Sylvia always turns up the volume. (Chapter 22)

Most recent reports tell of fires burning in streets and clashes between police and gangs of youths … (Chapter 35)

'You think it's funny that the police kill black people?' (Tufty, Chapter 36)

Summary

- De Waal uses her personal experience to present some of the realities of the care system.
- The novel is set at the start of Margaret Thatcher's government.
- 1981 was a year of civil unrest, which presaged the turbulent events of the 1980s to come.
- Race and racial disadvantage was a key topic in 1981.
- Many people saw the wedding of Charles and Diana in 1981 as a cause for celebration.

Questions

QUICK TEST
1. How could De Waal's experiences influence the presentation of Leon as a character?
2. What does De Waal want to show us about the care system?
3. How do we see racial divisions in the text?
4. Who was prime minister of the UK in 1981?
5. What event was seen by some as a cause for national celebration?

EXAM PRACTICE
When Leon asks a police officer for help, the police officer is incredibly racist to him. Why has De Waal included this in the novel? Using one or more of the 'Key quotations to learn', link this to the social and historical context.

Historical Context   35

Setting and Context: Literary Context

You must be able to: understand and comment on how the novel relates to other texts.

In what sense is the novel a bildungsroman?

De Waal uses a typical chronological structure, albeit with some use of flashback. This is typical of the **bildungsroman** narrative style. A bildungsroman is a coming-of-age story, where a child or young person goes through trials and difficulties that bring them into adult life. In regard to this text, while the events of the novel cover just over a year in Leon's life, the rather traumatic nature of the events often make it seem like a longer period of time. However, it is important to remember that Leon starts the text as an eight year old and has his tenth birthday late in the book.

Another well-known coming-of-age novel is Harper Lee's *To Kill a Mockingbird* (1960). This also has racial discrimination as a major theme. It is told in the first person (not the third person, like *My Name is Leon*) from the perspective of an eight-year-old girl, so it has some similarities to *My Name is Leon*. Meera Syal's *Anita and Me* (1996) is also told in the first person and has racism as a theme. While having a certain amount in common with De Waal's novel, these other texts combine the child's perspective with an element of their adult characters looking back on themselves as children, with an adult understanding. *My Name is Leon*'s special achievement is telling the story in the third person, but entirely from Leon's viewpoint, and without the element of adult understanding.

What is literary realism and how is it used in the novel?

Literary realism is a style of text that attempts to portray life directly and realistically, without any supernatural, fantastical or allegorical elements. Literary realism was first used in the Victorian era as a means of showing life 'as it is' for the lower classes. Charles Dickens is often seen as the pioneer of this literary movement. De Waal, when writing about a working-class mixed-race boy, also uses this style of literature to give as realistic an account as she can of the lives of children in the care system. It is also important to note that a key feature of literary realism is social commentary – the use of a direct and realistic writing style is meant to force the reader to confront unpleasant social realities without the distractions of fantastic or romanticised elements. We can contrast *My Name is Leon* with texts such as George Orwell's novel *Animal Farm* or J. B. Priestley's play *An Inspector Calls*, which use allegory, metaphor and elements of the supernatural to convey the writer's view on society.

While De Waal's text is not overtly political, as *Animal Farm* and *An Inspector Calls* are, she does show us the struggles of life in the early 1980s. She passes comment on the Royal Wedding between Charles and Diana and the hunger strikes by imprisoned IRA members, as well as presenting the Handsworth Riots and the police brutality endured by young Black men. This social commentary, while not always at the forefront of the text, is evident throughout it.

Key Quotations to Learn

- 'Because he's a baby, a white baby. And you're not.' (Maureen, Chapter 9)
- The wedding and then the riots and the Irishman that starved himself to death … (Chapter 24)
- 'I saw some policemen today and they were fighting with two black men.' (Leon, Chapter 27)
- Sylvia's friends talk about riots in another city and the Irishmen that are dying on a hunger strike. (Chapter 30)

Summary

- The novel is a bildungsroman – a coming-of-age story – and can be compared with *To Kill a Mockingbird* and *Anita and Me*.
- De Waal's novel is unusual in its use of third person to tell a story entirely from a child's viewpoint.
- De Waal uses literary realism to show life as it is. This technique creates an unflinching portrayal of life and avoids fantasy and idealisation.

Sample analysis

Maureen's direct comment to Leon, 'Because he's a baby, a white baby. And you're not', serves as a reminder of the racism and prejudice that was rife in the early 1980s. However, what is key is the direct nature of Maureen's language. De Waal ensures that Maureen's tone is very matter-of-fact, staying true to the literary realism style of literature rather than having Maureen speak in figurative language. Her assertion that Jake's adoption is mainly because of his youth and race serves as a poignant reminder of the attitudes of that time. Her direct language educates the reader as much as Leon.

Questions

QUICK TEST
1. Why might a writer use literary realism?
2. What social classes does literary realism usually focus on?
3. What is one of the political events that is mentioned in the text?
4. Who was one of the English pioneers of literary realism?
5. Name one thing that realism reveals about life in the UK in the 1980s.

EXAM PRACTICE
'Literary realism portrays life as it is.' How far do you agree with this comment regarding *My Name is Leon*?

Characters: Leon

You must be able to: explore how the character of Leon is presented.

Who is Leon?

Leon is the protagonist of the novel. The novel's title is a proclamation of his identity. Leon is intelligent, observant and responsible. All these characteristics are revealed in Chapter 5, when the reader sees him caring for Jake: 'Leon has a good system. It took him a few weeks to get it just right …' He notices what the baby needs, turns it into a system and gets on with it.

Leon has a mixture of wide-eyed innocence and maturity. His innocence shows, for example, in his fantasising to Sylvia about his parents' garden (Chapter 18). His maturity adds an element of pathos, as it has developed as a result of his difficult life so far. As the novel develops, Leon becomes further disillusioned as all of his family are taken away from him. His father may be in prison, his mother becomes institutionalised and Jake gets adopted. The one constant in Leon's life is his adoration of his brother Jake, which is heartbreaking, as we know that Jake will not come back. Chapter 38 begins with 'Inside Leon's body, everything is mixed up.' This helps to represent his state of confusion. He feels angry towards Social Services; he wants to rescue Jake, and to an extent he wants to rescue and parent his own mother.

How does Leon show his emotional disturbance?

Leon steals throughout the text. This could be due to him wanting to assert his autonomy. Stealing enables him to affect adults in ways that he is unable to do legitimately. His stealing also comes from a need for survival – he first steals when Carol is unwell and there is no food in the house. His nightmares also reveal the emotional toll that his situation has placed upon him. In Chapter 11, he dreams of fighting an evil monster. This could be a representation of the fight he has to have against Social Services – he is fighting a battle that he can never truly win. Leon's stealing is also an expression of his anger against how he has been treated. He even steals from those who have helped him.

What relationships help Leon to survive?

As Carol's mental state declines, she is less and less able to give him what he needs. His father, Byron, has long since left the family and is not a factor in Leon's daily life. Hence, Tufty becomes a father figure to him, showing him kindness and helping him to grow plants on the allotments. Mr Devlin also becomes a father figure. Both men collectively help Leon escape from the riot in Chapter 39.

Carol's place in Leon's life is gradually taken by Maureen, and then to a lesser extent by her sister, Sylvia. Leon responds to their firm guidance and especially to Maureen's affection. He also responds well to Sylvia's quirky sense of humour.

Key Quotations to Learn

'My. Name. Is. Leon.' (Chapter 2)
'My mum and dad have a massive garden.' (Chapter 18)
Inside Leon's body, everything is mixed up. (Chapter 38)

Summary

- Leon is the protagonist of the text.
- The reader witnesses his coming-of-age, as well as his turmoil.
- Leon represents the children who are ignored by society and by the system.
- He steals to provide for himself and Jake, and to give himself a sense of autonomy.
- When Carol is unable to care for him, Leon finds nurturing from Maureen, Sylvia, Tufty and Mr Devlin.

Sample Analysis

The opening of Chapter 38 states 'Inside Leon's body, everything is mixed up.' Here, the narrative voice allows us to delve into his inner psyche, where his mind is presented as messy and uncertain. Perhaps the adjective 'mixed' is used to emphasise his frustrated and confused mindset. What is fascinating is that De Waal distinguishes this as being inside his body, rather than inside his mind. This could be De Waal hinting at the physical effects of his mental anguish.

Questions

QUICK TEST
1. What does Leon's 'good system' show?
2. What wrongdoing does Leon frequently commit throughout the text?
3. What is the one constant in Leon's life?
4. Who does Leon particularly come to see as a paternal figure?
5. What aspect of Sylvia's character does Leon relate to?

EXAM PRACTICE
'Leon is a paradoxical character. He is never entirely good or bad.' Using one or more of the 'Key quotations to learn', write a paragraph explaining whether you agree with this statement.

Characters: Carol

You must be able to: understand and analyse the significance of Carol's character.

Why is Carol's physical appearance important in the novel?

A key feature of Carol's character is her physical appearance. She is often described as beautiful at the start of the text, however, as her mental health deteriorates, so does her appearance. In Chapter 14, after a period of absence, Leon observes that Carol's 'teeth and her fingers are yellowy brown like mustard and her cheeks go in like a skeleton.' While the reader, like Leon, is never fully privy to what is happening with Carol's treatment, the image is stark, especially in comparison to her beauty in the earlier chapters. It is almost as if Carol has begun to waste away, both physically and emotionally.

How is Carol presented as irresponsible?

Carol is presented as irresponsible and rather fickle. When she asks, 'Can I have that photo of my baby?' and takes away Leon's only photograph of Jake in Chapter 14, we realise that she does not understand or care how her actions affect Leon.

Carol allowing Leon to call her by her first name, rather than 'mum', may indicate that she is not fully committed to a maternal role and that she wants to separate herself from the responsibilities that come with parenthood. This contrasts sharply with Maureen, who has a 'Best Mum' spoon and whose identity is centred around how much she understands children.

Carol's appearances throughout the text are fleeting to represent her sporadic presence in Leon's life.

How is Carol presented as vulnerable?

Carol's vulnerability is a key feature of her character. She often appears wounded, as if she is hurt both physically and emotionally. It is important to note that the last time we see Carol in a happy mood is in Chapter 3, where she speaks about Jake's father. She explains that he 'forgot' about her due date, however, due to Tina's silence, the subtext is clear that he is ignoring and avoiding Carol. We can also see her as vulnerable when her mental and physical health deteriorate to the point where she cannot look after herself. This is the reason for the decline in her physical appearance and, despite her failure to provide Leon with the care that he needs throughout the novel, it may cause some sympathy in the reader.

Key Quotations to Learn

'… you're a proper beautiful bird but you've got a brain like a rusty motor.' (Tony, Chapter 4)

'Can I have that photo of my baby?' (Carol, Chapter 14)

Her teeth and her fingers are yellowy-brown like mustard and her cheeks go in like a skeleton. (Chapter 14)

'I can't look after you properly, you know that, don't you?' (Carol, Chapter 41)

Summary

- Carol is beautiful and therefore attractive to men at the start of the text.
- Carol is characterised as being too mentally unwell to parent her children.
- She often ignores her responsibilities as a mother.
- She is unrealistic and naïve.
- As the text develops, Carol's mental health and physical appearance deteriorate.

Sample Analysis

When Carol says 'I can't look after you properly, you know that, don't you?', this moment is cathartic not only for Leon, but also for the reader. It feels like Carol is finally admitting what both Leon and the reader have been aware of for most of the text – that Carol is unable to be a mother. Having her admit this almost provides a sense of relief and completion. By using a question, she is inviting Leon to also come to terms with her inadequacies as a parent.

Questions

QUICK TEST
1. What does Carol let Leon call her?
2. What does Carol take from Leon when she visits him at Maureen's house?
3. How does Carol physically change during the novel?
4. What does Carol finally admit to Leon?
5. What do her fleeting appearances in the novel represent?

EXAM PRACTICE
Using one or more of the 'Key quotations to learn', write a paragraph explaining how Carol is represented as a selfish and immature character.

Characters: Maureen

You must be able to: understand and analyse the significance of Maureen's character in the novel.

How is Maureen contrasted with Carol?

Maureen is in many ways juxtaposed with Carol. In Chapter 6, she proclaims 'I've got an eye for kids.' The description of her hair as looking like a 'flaming halo' could be symbolic of her being Leon's guardian angel, a character who looks after him, shows him undeniable love and is honest. De Waal's own mother may have been an inspiration for the character of Maureen, as she was a foster parent. Maureen is a very experienced foster parent, having cared for numerous children over the years. She says, with justification, that she knows a lot about children: 'Do you think there is anyone that knows more about children than me?' (Chapter 11). Even when Maureen is unwell, she still cares about Leon. Sylvia is overheard in Chapter 30 saying that Maureen was 'screaming blue murder' from her hospital bed to ensure that Leon got a card and photograph from Jake. Again, this reiterates her absolute love and her sense of justice and certainty.

How does Maureen treat Leon?

A key feature of Maureen's relationship with Leon is her willingness to listen to him. During their first meeting, in Chapter 6, she asks Leon about Jake, saying, 'You tell me what he likes and doesn't like so I don't get it wrong.' She also writes down all of Leon's comments, showing him the respect that he probably feels he hasn't had before. She then says, 'You've been really helpful' and makes it clear that she feels that Leon did a very good job of looking after Jake. She treats Leon almost like an equal, rather than purely as a child. She also learns what he likes so she can give him good presents.

How are the changes in Maureen's health presented?

The deterioration in Maureen's health happens very quickly. In Chapter 13, she gets 'a tight chest' when going to visit Sylvia. However, we realise that something more significant may be occurring. In Chapter 15, Maureen has to be rushed to hospital. It is important to note that Leon saves her life by getting an ambulance, in a similar way to his saving his mother's life by fetching Tina. De Waal chooses not to have Maureen appear much in the text during her stay in the hospital; we only see and hear about her sporadically, making us miss her just as much as Leon does.

Key Quotations to Learn

'That's me, Maureen, and I've got an eye for kids.' (Maureen, Chapter 6)
… her fuzzy red hairstyle looks like a flaming halo. (Chapter 6)
'You'll have lovely dreams tonight, Leon, love.' (Maureen, Chapter 7)
'… I think about you and I care for you and I love you.' (Maureen, Chapter 11)

Summary

- Maureen is the opposite of Carol.
- She is kind, yet firm and honest.
- Maureen listens properly to Leon.
- Key to Maureen's identity are her maternal instincts.
- She is a very experienced foster parent.

Sample Analysis

After her prolonged absence from the text due to illness, both the reader and Leon are delighted to see Maureen return in Chapter 35. Her perceptive comment that Leon has 'gone a bit quiet' once again highlights her emotional intelligence. Maureen is able to glean, from a very brief interaction with Leon, that there has been a shift in his disposition. This allows De Waal to contrast her with Sylvia who, despite her best efforts, is oblivious.

Questions

QUICK TEST
1. What does Maureen ensure that Leon gets on his birthday?
2. Who is a possible inspiration for the character of Maureen?
3. What does Maureen feel that she knows a lot about?
4. What is the first symptom of Maureen's illness?
5. What is the narrative effect of the reader not seeing much of Maureen while she is in hospital?

EXAM PRACTICE
Using one or more of the 'Key quotations to learn', write a paragraph explaining whether Maureen and Carol are direct opposites to each other.

Characters: Sylvia

You must be able to: understand and analyse the significance of Sylvia's character.

How is Sylvia and Leon's relationship initially presented?

Sylvia, Maureen's older sister, is an ambiguous character. At first, she is presented in an antagonistic manner and as a poor substitute for Maureen. She only finds herself caring for Leon because Maureen has to go into hospital and because she feels grateful to Leon for phoning for an ambulance. She even seems to exclude Leon, often referring to 'me and Mo'.

Chapter 16 begins with a list of things that Leon does not like and these are primarily to do with Sylvia and her home. She is also not as overtly maternal and caring as Maureen. However, she does seem to care about Leon, admitting to him in Chapter 28, 'We get on. I like you and you like me.' There is an element of dramatic irony here, as at this point Leon does not really like Sylvia. However, this moment is a turning point in the development of their relationship.

How do Leon and Sylvia eventually bond?

Sylvia shows her characteristic quirky humour, and some understanding of Leon, when in Chapter 23 she offers to bring him a picnic in the park, adding, 'Bet you'd rather have your nails dipped in acid.'

In Chapter 27, she tells Leon a long funny story about a rabbit. It is typical of Sylvia that it is a story that some adults (probably including Maureen) would say was inappropriate for a child. Also, it seems telling that both this and her story about the pig with the wooden leg (Chapter 30) are only funny because of someone being cruel to someone gullible. It is as if she sees the world as harsh but sees the humour in that. However, her humour works for Leon, and the pair of them end up laughing so much that they are 'on the bed together, rolling from side to side'. This becomes a bonding moment. Leon begins to understand Sylvia's idiosyncrasies, and the reader does too.

Sylvia admits that she got married very young. In Chapter 32, she says that she was 'fourteen when I went to work and seventeen when I got married. I was only a bloody child.' Perhaps she sees a similarity between herself and Leon – both forced to grow up far earlier than they should have been, due to circumstances they cannot control.

How are Sylvia's vulnerabilities presented?

There is a fallibility to Sylvia. Leon sees her as old, but she makes an effort with her appearance, including dying her hair purple. In Chapter 34, after being stood up for a date, she speaks of going to the seaside, 'Me and Mo. Hastings. Or Rye', not realising what saying this may do to Leon. While she doesn't mean to be cruel, it does reveal a lack of awareness. It is also interesting that Sylvia gets involved in organising the street party to celebrate the Royal Wedding (Chapter 22). Unexpectedly, she has started a relationship with Mr Devlin at the end of the novel. Maureen comments to her: 'He's got you like a sixteen-year-old, that's what.'

Key Quotations to Learn

'She's all right, is Sylvie. Once you've known her fifty years.' (Maureen, Chapter 13)
'Bet you'd rather have your nails dipped in acid.' (Sylvia, Chapter 23)
'He's got you like a sixteen-year-old, that's what.' (Maureen, Chapter 42)

Summary

- At first, Sylvia has a somewhat antagonistic role in the text due to Leon's dislike of her.
- Her relationship with Leon grows as they get used to each other.
- After a while, Leon appreciates Sylvia's sense of humour.
- She gets excited about the street party to celebrate the Royal Wedding.

Sample Analysis

Chapter 16 opens with a list of Leon's dislikes and a recurring subject on this list of dislikes is Sylvia. Leon perceives Sylvia as a hindrance; her rather prickly demeanour contrasts with Maureen's warmth. There is an element of humour that De Waal employs with this list, however it also reveals Leon's rather immature and innocent perspective.

Questions

QUICK TEST
1. Why does Leon have to live with Sylvia?
2. What does Sylvia do that makes Leon feel excluded?
3. How do Leon and Sylvia eventually bond?
4. What do Sylvia's funny stories have in common?
5. Who is Sylvia in a relationship with at the end of the novel?

EXAM PRACTICE
Using one or more of the 'Key quotations to learn', write a paragraph explaining whether Sylvia is an antagonistic character.

Characters

Tufty Burrows

You must be able to: understand and analyse the significance of Tufty's character.

How does Tufty influence Leon?

A young Black man who becomes a surrogate father figure to Leon, Tufty is characterised by his warmth and his giving nature. Tufty does not seem to be embarrassed by his nickname, given to him ironically because he lost all his hair as a child. In many ways, he is the direct opposite of Leon's father, who is shown to be inconsistent and volatile. Tufty nicknames Leon 'Star', showing the warmth he has towards Leon almost immediately. He instantly gives Leon a cream soda in Chapter 17.

He surrounds himself with images of strong Black male heroes whose pictures are on the wall of his shed. His poetry shows his more sensitive side, again distancing him from any harmful stereotypes associated with Black men. In Chapter 23, he educates Leon on the music of 'King Tubby, Bob Marley, Dennis Brown' and many others, allowing Leon to have some connection with his roots. It is also Tufty who first teaches Leon about growing plants on the allotment.

How does De Waal use Tufty's character to present prejudice?

Despite Tufty having a rather gentle temperament, he also rightfully gets frustrated with the racial injustice he witnesses. In Chapter 27, while trying to reclaim a sense of power after the police intrude on his area of the allotment, he says, 'This is my land. My piece of the earth.' His moments of anger are always justified in the context of the novel. One of the most **visceral** moments of the text occurs when Tufty is assaulted and witnesses the beating of his friend by the police in Chapter 27. As Tufty yells 'Leave him! Leave him! He can't breathe!' during the violent beating of Castro, the reader witnesses a different dimension to Tufty's character. We see the fear and the constant threat that the police enforce.

However, Tufty is not always right in his angry judgements. He accuses Mr Devlin of victimising him racially by having his allotment taken away, when in fact it is probably because the allotment committee says Tufty's father has broken the rules by sub-letting it to Tufty. In addition, he virtually accuses Mr Devlin of being a paedophile because he has pictures of boys on his shed wall (his pupils in Brazil) and takes an innocent interest in Leon. He is also prejudiced towards Mr Devlin as an Irishman.

What is the significance of Tufty's poetry?

Tufty's poetry creates another dimension to his character. A lover of words, it is telling that the sentence from his poem 'Ode to Castro', 'We have dignity and worth', resonates so much with Leon that he repeats it when he goes home, and again to the policeman at the riot. The dignity that Tufty speaks of is, perhaps, something that Leon has been lacking in his life, particularly when he was separated from baby Jake and passed to different carers without being consulted.

Key Quotations to Learn

'You want a drink, Star? Come.' (Tufty, Chapter 17)
'Leave him! Leave him! He can't breathe.' (Tufty, Chapter 27)
'I don't want to be a warrior / I didn't come for war.' (Tufty, Chapter 33)
'… we don't bomb people in their beds like you Irish people.' (Tufty, Chapter 36)

Summary

- Tufty becomes a paternal figure to Leon.
- De Waal chooses to create a character devoid of racial stereotypes – he is both masculine and gentle, intellectual and caring.
- Tufty mentors Leon through the art of gardening.
- Tufty writes poetry.
- He wrongly accuses Mr Devlin of being a paedophile.

Sample Analysis

The inclusion of Tufty's poetry heightens the complexity of his character. His 'Ode to Castro' is a sensitive yet blistering **diatribe** on the cruelty of police brutality. The phrasing of 'I don't want to be a warrior' is a rebuttal to the role of the aggressor that Black men in society are often forced to inhabit. Rather, Tufty desires peace and a feeling of equality.

Questions

QUICK TEST
1. What kind of music does Tufty introduce Leon to?
2. What does Tufty give Leon when they first meet?
3. What does Tufty get angry at?
4. What does Tufty have on the wall of his shed?
5. How is he wrong about Mr Devlin?

EXAM PRACTICE
Using one or more of the 'Key quotations to learn', write a paragraph explaining why Tufty is an important character.

Characters

Mr Devlin (Victor)

You must be able to: analyse Mr Devlin's role in the text and his relationship with other characters.

What role does Mr Devlin play in the story?

Mr Devlin is known only by his surname for most of the novel, which fits his rather remote personality. He is at first an ambiguous but largely unsympathetic character, an authoritarian who officiously enforces the rules of the allotments, and reprimands Tufty – whom he addresses formally as 'Mr Burrows' – for cycling. He also objects to Leon being there, pointing a knife at him and insisting: 'Children aren't allowed' (Chapter 17). The image of the knife is threatening, and later the pictures of boys and the gun in his shed suggest that he harbours dangerous secrets. However, this is misleading – Mr Devlin is actually another victim of loneliness and loss, like Leon. He has lost his son, as Leon has lost his parents and brother. The suggestion of a romantic relationship with Sylvia at the end of the novel ensures that he, too, is given an unexpected happy ending.

How is Mr Devlin portrayed as vulnerable?

Mr Devlin clashes with Tufty, although, as an Irishman in England, he is also something of an outsider. After their first argument, Leon notices that 'He has a bit of a limp' and 'He's much older than Mr Burrows … but he looks strong.'

Although Mr Devlin is initially portrayed almost as a threat, he is also deeply vulnerable. He drinks whiskey alone in his shed. Moreover, in Chapter 18, he says, 'I used to be Señor Victor,' hinting at his past as a teacher in Brazil. He also says 'or Papa', indicating that he was once a father but is no longer one. It is telling that, after Leon repeats 'papa', Mr Devlin says 'Ah'; it is almost as if being called that fond name again reignites a lost part of his identity. This may transform the reader's unease and fear of Mr Devlin to sympathy, as we come to understand how Leon may represent the life that Mr Devlin has lost.

In Chapter 31, his carvings of boys are revealed to be depictions of his students in a school he ran with his wife in Brazil. It is also indicated that he lost his own child – he says 'It's my fault' and goes on to say, 'Always will be my fault. For ever and ever. Amen.' This religious language, an allusion to the Lord's Prayer that is central to Christian practice, may indicate the intensity of his sorrow and regret. He carries a burden of guilt. Leon's presence in his life may offer him at least some small chance of redemption.

Key Quotations to Learn

'Thinks he owns this place. So busy spying, he forgets to live his life.' (Tufty, Chapter 17)
Leon smells sour whiskey on Mr Devlin's breath. (Chapter 23)
… photographs of boys, lots of them, dozens … (Chapter 26)
'I was loved. They loved me.' (Mr Devlin, Chapter 31)

Summary

- Mr Devlin is a mysterious character who becomes a surrogate father figure to Leon.
- He likes to insist on the rules of the allotments.
- He is isolated and somewhat bad-tempered.
- He helps Tufty to save Leon from the police during the riot.
- He becomes part of Leon's found family, becoming involved with Sylvia.

Sample Analysis

Chapter 31 gives us insight into Mr Devlin's past. While not everything is stated, the reader becomes privy to the loss that Mr Devlin has suffered. De Waal employs the past tense with 'had' and 'loved'. The notion of him being loved, and part of a community, creates a real sense of sadness as it also shows the reader that he does not feel loved anymore.

Questions

QUICK TEST
1. What does Mr Devlin tell Tufty off for doing?
2. What does Mr Devlin have in his shed?
3. What do Mr Devlin's secrets turn out to be?
4. What do Mr Devlin's carvings depict?
5. With whom does Mr Devlin end up in a romantic relationship?

EXAM PRACTICE
Using one or more of the 'Key quotations to learn', write a paragraph explaining the role that Mr Devlin plays in the novel.

Themes: Isolation and Community

You must be able to: analyse which characters in the novel are isolated and why.

Who is isolated and why?

Leon becomes increasingly isolated as the text develops. Due to his mixed-race heritage, Leon is treated differently by society. The reader sees this most acutely in the racism he is shown by the policeman during the riot. A key feature of Leon's isolation is that he is a young person surrounded by adults, many of whom do not listen to him. One exception is the Zebra, a social worker who does make an effort with him. He mentions that the only person to tell him the truth is Maureen. He feels isolated at school and seems to want to seek comfort with other adults, in particular Tufty.

To some extent, Carol is also isolated. Her mental health means that she lacks meaningful relationships. For instance, her relationship with Tina seems to be more about the support that she gets from Tina, whether with money or with taking care of Leon. Her understanding of relationships, as shown by her relationships with men, particularly Jake's father, seems superficial. However, the reader does feel sorry for Carol, as her isolation makes her a victim as well.

Mr Devlin is also isolated. At first, the reader sees him as an unpleasant man who wants to tell others what to do, but it may be that his trust in rules is his way of coping with life. As he gradually gets to know Leon, the reader discovers that he had a son in Brazil and worked in a school there. De Waal never explains how he came to be living in England and never shows him relating in a friendly way to anyone else, until at the end of the novel he forms a romantic relationship with Sylvia.

Byron, while playing no part in the novel's action, feels completely isolated after the death of his mother in Antigua, despite having a son – Leon.

What are the effects of isolation?

One effect of Leon's isolation is his anger at the world around him, which makes him steal from adults and cause deliberate damage as a way of having power in the world. Another possible effect is misunderstanding. For example, Tufty and Mr Devlin have little understanding of each other and only reach any kind of mutual respect as a result of the riot. Tufty completely misunderstands Mr Devlin's pictures of boys and the attention he gives Leon, and Mr Devlin is more interested in making Tufty obey the rules than in finding out about his character.

How is community shown in the novel?

The opposite of isolation in the novel could be seen as community. The reader sees this, for example, when Tufty and other men get together at the allotments and play dominoes and share views, and in Sylvia meeting with friends to plan the Royal Wedding street party. Community is seen as something nurturing – almost an extension of family. The wedding is a social focal point that brings people together.

Key Quotations to Learn

'Leave me alone! Leave me alone!' (Carol, Chapter 5)
Carol keeps crying and going to the phone box, leaving Leon in charge ... (Chapter 5)
'You should have friends, Leon.' (Sylvia, Chapter 30)

Summary

- Leon's isolation stems from neglect and to some extent him being mixed race.
- Leon is a child in an adult world.
- When Leon loses Jake, he feels all the more isolated.
- Carol's loneliness is rooted in her mental illness.
- Community is seen as an antidote to isolation.

Sample Analysis

In Chapter 30, Sylvia states, 'You should have friends, Leon', due to there being no children at Leon's birthday party. There is a simplicity to Sylvia's language, as she states her understanding of Leon's pain. De Waal's use of the modal verb 'should' conveys that this is a suggestion. This could be De Waal showing a more nuanced aspect of Sylvia's character – while she understands that it would be healthy for Leon to have friends, she also realises the challenges he is facing. This is a moment where Sylvia's understanding of Leon's isolation creates a shift in the reader's perspective of her.

Questions

QUICK TEST
1. Which social worker listens to Leon?
2. Where did Mr Devlin have a son?
3. What causes Carol's isolation?
4. How is the Royal Wedding important to community in the novel?
5. What event brings Tufty and Mr Devlin together?

EXAM PRACTICE
Using one or more of the 'Key quotations to learn', write a paragraph explaining how De Waal uses the theme of isolation to create sympathy for the characters of Leon and Carol.

Isolation and Community

Themes: Race and Racialised Identity

You must be able to: analyse how the novel looks at race.

How does Leon view his own racial identity?

In Chapter 1, when speaking to baby Jake, Leon says: 'I look like my dad. Mum says he's coloured but Dad says he's black but they're both wrong because he's dark brown and I'm light brown.' This quotation reveals the innocence of Leon's outlook. He has a simplified view of his own racial identity, but he understands that he is different from both parents. Carol describing his father as 'coloured', which even in the 1980s had become an offensive term, shows that she is somewhat ignorant of race and racialised identity.

How does Leon's race affect how others treat him?

Leon is frequently called 'big for his age'. This could be interpreted as a presentation of the adultification of Black boys, whereby they are viewed as older than they really are and therefore treated in ways which would be unacceptable for children. The policeman who almost hits Leon with his truncheon probably thinks he is a teenager. A key aspect of racial identity is also evident in the differences between the treatment of Jake and Leon. When Maureen says in Chapter 9 that Jake gets adopted 'Because he's a baby, a white baby. And you're not', this spells out the situation clearly and honestly.

How does Tufty view racial identity?

De Waal uses the character of Tufty to explore racial identity in a more positive manner. Tufty, a young Black man whom Leon befriends at the allotments, becomes a paternal figure for him. His pride in his culture is shown in Chapter 18. The posters of Black men, 'one who looks like a king' (possibly Haile Selassie of Ethiopia) and another 'with his fist in the air', are representations of Black historical figures. While they are not named, the reader can guess that some are activists such as Malcolm X, Martin Luther King or Huey Newton. These images represent Tufty's pride in his Blackness. Later on, Leon even admits that, when he looks at Tufty, he thinks of his father. However, there is a much more threatening presentation of racial identity in the events of the Handsworth Riots. The violence and the beating and ultimate death of Castro show the difficulties that Black people faced in Britain in the 1980s.

Key Quotations to Learn

'Mum says he's coloured but Dad says he's black but they're both wrong because he's dark brown and I'm light brown.' (Leon, Chapter 1)

'Because he's a baby, a white baby. And you're not.' (Maureen, Chapter 9)

He looks big for his age, twelve or thirteen … (Chapter 17)

Summary

- Leon's racial identity adds to his feeling of isolation.
- As the only mixed-race person in his family, he often feels different.
- Black boys are often regarded as being older than they really are.
- Tufty becomes a means for Leon to understand his Black identity in a positive way.
- Tufty has pictures of his heroes on his shed wall.

Sample Analysis

Maureen's explanation that Jake is being adopted predominantly 'Because he's a baby, a white baby. And you're not' is one of the most brutal yet necessary statements in the novel. It not only tells the reader about Jake's and Leon's relative status, it also reveals Maureen's character as someone who will not shy away from hard discussions. She is blunt and direct to him because she loves and cares about him, not as a means to hurt him, which we would normally expect. Using the adjective 'white' helps to emphasise the main issue that separates Leon and Jake. Even though they are brothers, Jake's whiteness makes him more acceptable to prospective parents. Even though Leon also has white ancestry because of his mixed-race heritage, his primary racial identity is that of being Black.

Questions

QUICK TEST

1. What does Tufty have on the walls of his shed in the allotment?
2. What does Carol call Leon's father?
3. What are the two reasons Jake gets adopted?
4. Who almost hits Leon?
5. What does the beating and killing of Castro show?

EXAM PRACTICE

'The treatment of Leon shows that even children can be victims of racism, no matter how young they are.' Using one or more of the 'Key quotations to learn', write a paragraph explaining whether you agree with this statement.

Race and Racialised Identity

Themes: Family and Parenting

You must be able to: analyse how family is presented in the novel.

How is the concept of family presented in the opening chapters?
The first family the reader encounters is Leon, Carol and Jake. While this is not a traditional nuclear family, largely due to the absence of a father, Leon's love for his mother and his baby brother is undeniable. However, this family is in a precarious situation. Leon often has to look after himself and his younger brother. The boys' fathers take no responsibility for their sons.

How are Maureen and Sylvia part of Leon's family?
Maureen is deeply maternal and becomes Leon's substitute mother. She contrasts with Carol as she enjoys the domestic life, loves to feed people, both emotionally and physically, and is also very honest with Leon. Leon even admits that she's one of the few people who tell him the truth. Maureen's relationship with Sylvia, and the closeness they feel, also shows the beauty of family. Sylvia is less naturally maternal than Maureen, but her love for Maureen makes her agree to look after Leon, and she forms a bond with him, caring for him in her own way.

How is fatherhood presented in the novel?
Both Leon's and Jake's fathers are presented in rather negative ways. Leon's father is probably in prison and seems irresponsible. This is contrasted with Tufty, who becomes a surrogate father to Leon, showing him love and teaching him about gardening. Perhaps De Waal is suggesting that the concept of family is fluid. The final scene, with Leon in a house with Maureen, Sylvia, Tufty and Mr Devlin, shows us that Leon has found a functioning family: people who love him and show him care.

Leon's father Byron is absent from the events of the novel, although he appears in flashbacks and references made by other characters. Tina mentions that he's 'done a runner' and that he was 'inside for a bit', a reference to prison time. Leon's memories of his voice and his colloquialisms such as 'soon come' and 'neck-back' suggest his Caribbean ancestry. This is further acknowledged when Leon remembers the time he met his ailing grandmother who had 'a big map of Antigua' (a Caribbean island) in her living room. In fact, that vignette in Chapter 31 is very revealing about Leon's father. After his mother dies, he says, 'I got no one now. I got no one now. I got no one now.' There is a correlation here between Byron losing his mother and Leon losing Carol. Both of them feel alone and in need of support. There is also a connection with Mr Devlin, who seems to have lost a family in Brazil and is alone until he meets Leon and Sylvia.

Key Quotations to Learn

He's never heard his dad sound like a little boy. (Chapter 31)

'Wouldn't you like Jake to be in a family with a mum and dad of his own?' (Salma, Chapter 9)

'I got no one now. I got no one now. I got no one now.' (Byron, Chapter 31)

Leon likes it when they [Tufty and Mr Devlin] pretend to argue like they used to. (Chapter 42)

Summary

- The novel shows the reader that families can be formed in different ways.
- De Waal shows the painful effects of an absence of family.
- Byron deeply grieves his mother, seemingly unaware that he still has a son.
- Social Services are seen as sometimes ignoring the needs of families.

Sample Analysis

When Maureen asserts in Chapter 11 that 'you will see Jake again. He hasn't gone for ever', just like Leon, the reader is also hopeful. However, with each chapter that passes, De Waal indicates that seeing Jake again will never happen. The reader and Leon both experience the depths of their separation. Each chapter emphasises Leon's desperation to be reunited with his brother. When we finally do hear of Jake again, the typed letter and image pale in comparison with the real baby brother.

Questions

QUICK TEST
1. What do Leon's father and Jake's father have in common?
2. How does Byron appear in the novel?
3. Who becomes the main maternal figure in Leon's life?
4. How are Leon and his father seen as being similar?
5. Where did Mr Devlin have a family?

EXAM PRACTICE

'De Waal suggests that the concept of family cannot be defined.' Using one or more of the 'Key quotations to learn', write a paragraph explaining whether you agree.

Themes

Childhood

You must be able to: understand and analyse how De Waal presents childhood in the novel.

How do we see a child's perspective in the novel?

A key feature of the text is that the reader sees the world through a child's perspective. Leon is nearly nine years old at the beginning of the novel. However, his responsibilities and experiences are beyond his years. There are moments when Leon is undoubtedly mature for his age, such as in the early chapters when he takes on a semi-parental role with his little brother Jake. However, he still makes rash and emotionally charged decisions, for example when he expresses his anger by deliberately making a mess of Sylvia's bathroom (Chapter 28). De Waal shows us that Leon is in a state of transit. Physically, he appears much older and is consistently described as being big for his age. Mentally, he has the capacity to be empathetic and make plans, but he does not understand the dangers that await him in the world. His trusting nature and innocence are possibly most evident in his standoff with a police officer during the riots in Chapter 38.

How does Leon demonstrate the imaginative life of a child?

Despite his willingness to take responsibility for his baby brother, and even his mother, Leon's imaginative life shows that he is still very much a child. He plays with toys, especially his Action Man dolls, and he imagines that when Jake is old enough, they will 'play together, soldiers and Action Man' (Chapter 1). He also enjoys fantasies of being a brave soldier and being able to defend himself. For example, he imagines defending himself against Jake's father: 'If he has got a gun and he tries to shoot, Leon will kick the door off the hinges and attack him before he can pull the trigger' (Chapter 4). Later, he pursues a childishly unrealistic plan to find Jake, which begins with him climbing out of the window: 'Leon has done a brave thing. He's a burglar. He's James Bond' (Chapter 36).

What kind of childhood does Leon have?

Leon's childhood is characterised as being dysregulated. It is noted early on in the novel that this is not the first time he has been fostered. He thinks that 'nobody needs to know that Carol is ill again' (Chapter 5) – the adverb 'again' suggests that Carol's mental health has resulted in Leon being placed in foster care before. His determination to avoid this is what spurs his resolution to look after Jake and Carol. At one point, he realises that his mum has 'wet the bed again' (Chapter 5) which reveals how the roles of parent and child have been subverted. It is also telling that Tina informs the social workers that she thinks Leon's 'been in care a couple of times' (Chapter 5), revealing that Leon's childhood prior to the events of the novel has also been filled with instability and uncertainty.

Key Quotations to Learn

When Leon's brother is older they're going to play together, soldiers and Action Man. (Chapter 1)

He was creeping through the jungle with his men with a rifle and a gun and a secret knife in his sock. (Chapter 7)

He looks big for his age, twelve or thirteen, and now, with his new bike, he could even be fourteen. (Chapter 17)

Summary

- Leon is often treated differently due to his 'older' appearance.
- De Waal tells the story from Leon's childlike perspective.
- Leon has the imaginative life of a child, playing with his Action Man dolls and fantasising about being a brave soldier.
- There is a constant tension between Leon's apparent maturity and his innocence and ignorance.

Sample Analysis

The fairly innocuous comment of 'you're nice and big for your age' is made by a minor character, a nurse in Chapter 1. However, this commentary on age and Leon's supposedly older appearance is a key feature of the text. Perhaps De Waal is suggesting that Leon's appearance makes other people ignore his innocence and his need for protection.

Questions

QUICK TEST
1. How does Leon show responsibility?
2. What are Leon's favourite toys?
3. How does Leon typically see himself in his fantasies?
4. What popular film hero does Leon identify with?
5. What key information does Tina give the social workers about Leon's childhood?

EXAM PRACTICE
Using one or more of the 'Key quotations to learn', write a paragraph explaining how De Waal uses the theme of childhood to create empathy for Leon.

Themes

Mental Health and Social Services

You must be able to: understand and explain the role that mental health plays in the novel.

How is Carol's mental health presented?

The text looks at how mental health affects not only the sufferer, but also those around them. Chapter 3 begins, 'Leon has begun to notice the things that make his mum cry'. De Waal then lists a series of things that overwhelm Carol. In Chapter 4, Jake's father says she has 'a brain like a rusty motor'. This simile shows the ignorance that many had regarding mental health. The text is set in 1981, two years before the 1983 Mental Health Act in which assessment and treatment were given a basic foundation in British law. Social attitudes and healthcare provision for mental health were harsh at this time.

Another insight into mental health treatment comes when Leon finds a letter referring to Carol's psychiatric assessment. Its language is detached and medical, consisting of a list of her symptoms: '… including anxiety, restlessness, stupor and transient mood swings into hypomania' (Chapter 12).

How is Leon's mental health presented?

Leon's nightmares, his stealing and his angry outbursts could be read as manifestations of emotional disturbance caused by neglect. For instance, in Chapter 12, he vandalises Salma's belongings because he is frustrated by his situation. In Chapter 14, witnessing the deterioration of Carol's mental health, Leon suppresses all of his anger, saying 'under his breath, so Maureen won't hear, all the bad words he has stored up all day'. His desire to please his mother seems to cause him anger and frustration. In Chapter 38, during the riots, Leon is described as wanting to 'fight'. This may be a manifestation of his suppressed anger. He is also described as being 'mixed up' (Chapter 38). His tensions are too challenging for a child to comprehend or cope with, but he is too young to articulate this.

What role do Social Services play in relation to mental health?

Social Services are involved in organising Carol's care and treatment, and the care of her children. At times they are seen negatively, but not always. The Zebra, nicknamed this due to her 'black hair with white underneath' (Chapter 5), is Leon's main social worker. At first, he distrusts her, believing that she is only 'pretending to care' about him and his mother. However, she later goes beyond her role, getting him a BMX bike. She also displays honesty and professionalism. When Leon suggests in Chapter 16 that he could look after Carol, she tells him frankly that this is not a good idea because he is a child and Carol 'needs a lot of support'. She also remembers his birthday (Chapter 30), unlike his mother. While the Zebra appears only sporadically, she is consistently there, unlike Carol. De Waal could be acknowledging the good that many social workers do.

Key Quotations to Learn

… Carol keeps crying and going to the phone box … (Chapter 5)
How long will it be for her to get better? When is she coming back for him? (Chapter 14)
Earring puts his pen down and Leon knows every word that he's going to say. (Chapter 28)

Summary

- De Waal shows the effects of a parent's poor mental health on a child.
- Mental health is a very complex issue, as shown by the stages of Carol's decline.
- Carol's deterioration leads to frustration for Leon.
- Social Services are seen as sometimes uncaring, but the Zebra is portrayed more positively.

Sample Analysis

Tony describes Carol as 'a proper beautiful bird but you've got a brain like a rusty motor'. This simile exposes Tony's lack of care, as well as his ignorance. The description also objectifies Carol and could be regarded as sexist. The adjective 'rusty' suggests that Carol's mental state is damaged. However, Tony's criticism is ironic as Carol's mental instability is partly due to his negligence, both as a father to Jake and as a romantic partner to her.

Questions

QUICK TEST
1. What does Leon begin to notice about Carol after she comes home with Jake?
2. What image does Tony use to describe Carol's brain?
3. How does Leon show his mental health issues?
4. How does De Waal reveal Carol's psychiatric assessment?
5. What does the Zebra give Leon?

EXAM PRACTICE
Using one or more of the 'Key quotations to learn', write a paragraph explaining how De Waal uses mental health issues to develop the characters of Leon and Carol.

The Exam: Tips and Assessment Objectives

You must be able to: understand how to approach the exam question and meet the requirements of the mark scheme.

Quick tips

- You will have a choice of two questions. Attempt the question that best matches your knowledge, the quotations you have memorised and the content you have revised.
- Make sure you understand what the question is asking you to do. Underline key words and pay attention to the bullet point prompts that come with your question.
- You should spend 45 minutes on your *My Name is Leon* response. Allow yourself five minutes to plan your answer so that there is a clear structure to your essay.
- Your first paragraph should be a thesis statement, outlining your argument and your overall response to the question. Your analytical paragraphs should then expand on the ideas from your thesis.
- Use quotations or references that link back to the question and are relevant.
- Keep your writing style clear and concise and ensure that each paragraph helps to build your answer to the question.
- It is a good idea to remember what the mark scheme is asking you to do.

AO1: Understand and respond to the text (12 marks)

AO1 is all about showing your understanding of the text and having a clear response to the question.

Lower	Middle	Upper
The essay has some good ideas that are mostly relevant. Some quotations and references are used to support the ideas.	A clear essay that always focuses on the exam question. Quotations and references support ideas effectively. The response refers to different points of the text.	This essay will be well-structured and have an element of critical analysis. The response will be able to weave ideas from across the text. Quotations and references will be well-chosen and thoughtful.

AO2: Analysing the effects of De Waal's language, form and structure (12 marks)

AO2 requires you to comment on how De Waal uses narrative structure, specific words and language devices to get her ideas across to the reader.

Lower	Middle	Upper
Identification of certain methods. There may be some comment on the effects that these methods have.	Explanation of De Waal's use of methods. Accurate use of terminology and an understanding of the intended effects of these methods.	Accuracy when discussing subject terminology, depth of analysis and a thorough exploration of the effects.

AO3: Understand the relationship between the novel and its context (6 marks)

For this part of the mark scheme, you need to show your understanding of how the characters or De Waal's ideas relate to the time the novel is set (1981) and even when the novel was written (2016).

Lower	Middle	Upper
Some awareness of how ideas in the novel link to its context.	References to relevant aspects of context show a clear understanding.	Exploration is linked to specific aspects of the novel's contexts to show a detailed understanding.

AO4: Written accuracy (4 marks)

You need to use accurate vocabulary, expression, punctuation and spelling. While this is only worth four marks, it could make a difference between a lower or higher grade.

Lower	Middle	Upper
Reasonable level of accuracy; errors do not get in the way of the essay making sense.	Good level of accuracy; vocabulary and sentences help to keep ideas clear.	Consistent high level of accuracy; vocabulary and sentences are used to make ideas clear and precise.

The Exam — Practice Questions

1. Explore how Leon's feelings of responsibility are presented in the novel.
   Write about:
   - how the writer presents Leon's sense of responsibility
   - how the writer presents Leon's character and relationships.

2. Explore how Maureen is presented as an important character in the novel.
   Write about:
   - how the writer presents Maureen's role and personality
   - how the writer shows her impact on Leon and others.

3. Explore how the character of Carol is presented in the novel.
   Write about:
   - how the writer presents Carol's actions and behaviour
   - how the writer uses Carol to explore key themes in the novel.

4. Explore how the impact of change on Leon's character is presented in the novel.
   Write about:
   - how the writer presents moments of change in Leon's life
   - how the writer shows change affecting Leon's development.

5. Explore how Tufty is presented as a significant influence on Leon.
   Write about:
   - how the writer presents Tufty's relationship with Leon
   - how the writer shows Tufty's importance in Leon's life.

6. Explore how the theme of identity is presented in the novel.
   Write about:
   - how the writer presents Leon's struggle with identity
   - how the writer uses other characters and events to explore identity.

7. Explore how the effects of racism and discrimination are presented in the novel.
   Write about:
   - how the writer presents racism and discrimination
   - how the writer shows their impact on characters in the novel.

8. Explore how the theme of family is presented in the novel.
   Write about:
   - how the writer presents Leon's experience of family
   - how the writer uses relationships to explore the idea of family.

9. Explore how the theme of belonging is presented in the novel.
   Write about:
   - how the writer shows Leon's search for belonging
   - how the writer uses characters and settings to explore this theme.
10. Explore how the theme of loss is presented throughout the novel.
    Write about:
    - how the writer presents loss through Leon's experiences
    - how the writer shows the emotional impact of loss on characters.
11. Explore how Kit de Waal presents Leon's relationship with Jake in the novel.
    Write about:
    - how the writer presents Leon's feelings about his brother
    - how the writer shows the impact of their separation.
12. Explore how the theme of social care and the care system is presented in the novel.
    Write about:
    - how the writer presents Leon's experiences in care
    - how the writer uses characters and events to explore the care system.
13. Explore how Kit de Waal presents the theme of hope in the novel.
    Write about:
    - how the writer presents hopeful moments for Leon
    - how the writer contrasts hope with struggle or despair.
14. Explore how Leon's emotions are presented in the novel.
    Write about:
    - how the writer shows Leon dealing with difficult emotions
    - how the writer uses language and structure to reflect his emotional journey.
15. Explore how the character of Sylvia is presented in the novel.
    Write about:
    - how the writer presents Sylvia's behaviour and attitudes
    - how the writer uses Sylvia to influence the story or develop themes.
16. Explore how the theme of justice and fairness is presented in the novel.
    Write about:
    - how the writer shows Leon's sense of what is fair or unfair
    - how the writer uses events or characters to explore this theme.
17. Explore how male role models are presented in the novel.
    Write about:
    - how the writer presents the men in Leon's life
    - how the writer explores their influence on Leon's identity and choices.
18. Explore how Kit de Waal presents the theme of growing up in the novel.
    Write about:
    - how the writer shows Leon's development as he grows older
    - how the writer uses challenges and experiences to shape his character.

The Exam
Planning a Character Question Response

You must be able to: understand what a character-based question is asking you and prepare your response.

How might an exam question on character be phrased?
A typical character question will read like this:

> Explore how the character of Maureen is presented as a maternal figure.
>
> Write about:
> - what Maureen does and the reasons for her actions
> - the way De Waal presents Maureen throughout the text. (30 marks + 4 AO4 marks)

How do I work out what to do?
Work out the focus of the question. In this case, it's about Maureen as a maternal figure. A good way to think about character questions is to ask 'why is this character significant and what makes them significant?' and to address the question that way.

'How' and 'why' are important elements. For AO1, you need to show an understanding of the way Maureen's character is presented and why she is presented as a maternal figure. Think about the purpose that Maureen serves in the text. For AO2, the word 'how' means you need to analyse the way De Waal's use of language, structure and form contribute to the reader's understanding of Maureen's character. While it is good to have quoted evidence, you can also use clear references to specific parts of the novel.

You also need to remember to link your answer to context to achieve the AO3 marks, and to write accurately to gain the full AO4 marks for spelling, punctuation and grammar.

How can I plan my essay?
You have 45 minutes to answer this question. Although this doesn't seem like a long time, it is incredibly important to spend the first five to ten minutes writing a quick plan. This will help you to focus your thoughts and produce a well-structured essay. You should then spend 30–35 minutes writing, leaving yourself around five minutes for checking your answer.

Try to think of five or six ideas; each of these can become a paragraph. If possible, add a quick reminder of a quote or context you could write about, but focus on getting the main paragraph ideas down. For a character question, a good idea is to number each paragraph to make sure that you're writing about the character chronologically through the text.

You can plan in whatever way you find most useful. Some students like to just make a quick list of points and then re-number them into a logical order or to create a flowchart. Spider diagrams are particularly popular; look at the example on the next page.

> Beginning: Maureen is presented as the antithesis of Carol. 'That's me, Maureen, and I've got an eye for kids.' Context: De Waal's own mother was a foster carer.

> Maureen's physical attributes link to her wider role as a saviour for Leon. 'her fuzzy red hairstyle looks like a flaming halo'

Explore how the character of Maureen is presented as a maternal figure.

> Maureen is characterised as a nurturer. 'It's impossible to choose a favourite dinner at Maureen's house.'

> Maureen is shown to be honest but caring. 'Because he's a baby, a white baby. And you're not.' Context: mixed-race people faced significant prejudice in 1981.

Summary

- Make sure you understand the focus of the question (AO1).
- Analyse how the writer conveys ideas through the use of language, structure and form (AO2).
- Link ideas to social and historical context (AO3).
- Ensure your writing is clear and that you use accurate spelling, punctuation and grammar (AO4).

Questions

QUICK TEST
1. What key skills do you need to include in your answers?
2. What timing should you use?
3. Why is planning important?

EXAM PRACTICE
Plan a response to the following exam question:
How and why does Carol change in *My Name is Leon*?
Write about:
- what Carol does and her reasons for her actions
- how De Waal presents Carol throughout the novel.   (30 marks + 4 AO4 marks)

Planning a Character Question Response

The Exam

Grade 5 Annotated Response

Explore how the character of Maureen is presented as a maternal figure.

Write about:
- what Maureen does and the reasons for her actions
- the way De Waal presents Maureen throughout the text. (30 marks + 4 AO4 marks)

The character of Maureen is used by De Waal to contrast with Leon's mother's lack of maternal instinct. (1) Perhaps De Waal was inspired by her own mother, who fostered many children, as Maureen is a symbol of love and care. (2)

Maureen is described in Chapter 6 as having a 'fuzzy red hairstyle' which 'looks like a flaming halo'. (3) The use of the halo simile could be symbolic of Maureen's role as a guardian angel to Leon. (4) She is a character who shows him love and care in his time of need. (5) Maureen's large and energetic personality is also steeped in her knowledge of children; she says 'I've got an eye for kids', as well as having a spoon in her kitchen that says 'Best Mum'. Each of these attributes is used to represent her as maternal and starkly different from the more relaxed and neglectful Carol.

Another key feature of Maureen that could be seen as maternal is how much she feeds Leon. She gives him a range of foods. Chapter 8 begins with 'It's impossible to choose a favourite dinner at Maureen's house.' The adjective 'impossible' emphasises the quantity and quality of food at Maureen's house, which is starkly different from the lack of food that Carol provides. (6)

(7) Another key feature of Maureen is her honesty. In Chapter 9, when Jake's adoption is approaching, she explains to Leon that this is mainly due to Jake being 'a baby, a white baby. And you're not.' The bluntness of her language is alarming, but not due to it being cruel. Instead, we, like Leon, appreciate her honesty. Later on, in Chapter 28, Leon refers to her as 'the only one who has never lied'. Using the adverb 'only' emphasises the importance of Maureen's role and shows how significantly different she is from every other adult figure in the novel. (8)

(9) To conclude, Maureen is a character who, while not perfect, represents the undeniable love that Leon needs. When it becomes obvious that Leon will continue to live with Maureen at the end, the reader feels a sense of relief as we know that he will be safe and looked after. (10)

1. The question is instantly addressed in the opening sentence. AO1
2. Use of context is added with relevance and clarity. AO3
3. The evidence from the text is both relevant and embedded well into the writing. AO1/AO4
4. The mention of what the quote could mean helps to develop this paragraph. AO2
5. Some interpretation of the quotation is mentioned here. AO2
6. The comparison between Carol and Maureen helps show that this candidate has considered the entire text. AO1/AO2
7. The paragraphs each have a specific and clear focus. AO1
8. Use of subject terminology is accurate and aids the development of the essay. AO2
9. Good use of discourse marker to ensure clarity. AO1/AO4
10. The conclusion helps to complete the argument and ends with a sense of interpretation. AO1

Questions

EXAM PRACTICE
Choose a paragraph of this essay. Read it through a few times and then try to improve it. You might:
- change or edit the quotations used to improve relevance
- analyse a quotation with more detail
- improve the range of analysis – go deeper with different ideas
- improve expression with more sophisticated vocabulary
- connect more analysis to the paragraph.

The Exam | Grade 7+ Annotated Response

Explore how the character of Maureen is presented as a maternal figure.

Write about:

- what Maureen does and the reasons for her actions
- the way De Waal presents Maureen throughout the text. (30 marks + 4 AO4 marks)

In a text where several of the adult characters are presented as neglectful, Maureen becomes a symbol of maternal love and care. (1) De Waal does not deify Maureen, but rather employs a realism that makes her the emotional centre of the text. (2)

Our first introduction to Maureen in Chapter 6 plunges us into an environment of warmth and stability. (3) This obviously juxtaposes with the chaotic nature of Carol's home. Maureen is described as having 'a fuzzy red hairstyle' which 'looks like a flaming halo'. Here, De Waal uses a myriad of symbols to convey the warmth and resilience that will characterise her throughout the text. For instance, the use of 'halo' is celestial imagery, perhaps linking Maureen with a supernatural higher power. (4) This is further conveyed with the religious imagery of Jesus in her kitchen. Perhaps De Waal is suggesting that Maureen will guide Leon during this difficult journey. Furthermore, by using the colour imagery of red, her passion and joy for children becomes evident. Maureen's life is centred around children, which once again contrasts with the more self-centred Carol. (5)

(6) A key feature of Maureen is her propensity for feeding Leon. While on the surface, this could be seen as a purely nurturing characteristic, there are moments where we question the role that food plays in Maureen's life. In Chapter 8, Leon's refusal of her food becomes a symbol of rebellion. The food is described as 'sitting in his belly like a bag of sand'. There is a heaviness to Maureen's care and, while never negative, it does seem to create an emotional and physical burden on Leon. (7)

A further key feature of Maureen's character is her candour. When Jake is about to be adopted, she admits to Leon that it is due to him being 'a white baby'. (8) This moment reveals a lot about Maureen's character; her admitting that whiteness makes him an attractive candidate for adoption, particularly compared to Leon's mixed-race heritage, is one of the most challenging moments in the text. However, it becomes almost cathartic for both Leon and the reader, as we admire her honesty. Later on, in Chapter 28, Leon describes her as 'the only one who has never lied' to him. The adverb 'never' emphasises the differences between Maureen and the other adults in Leon's life. (9)

In conclusion, Maureen's character seems to be a means for De Waal to showcase the heroism of foster parents. When Maureen is unwell and absent from the text, it is telling that not only does Leon miss her presence, but so does the reader. We come to realise that her significance is that she represents the importance of love in the text and also educates the reader on the true meaning of family. (10)

1. The opening of this essay instantly shows a level of focus on the question. AO1
2. There is an introduction of a sort of argument here as well as a strong critical interpretation. AO1
3. The topic sentence not only makes a statement, but there is also an understanding of De Waal's reasons for her choice. AO1
4. Analysis of quotation is detailed and uses high-level vocabulary accurately and to develop the answer. AO2/AO4
5. The analysis is detailed and considers more than one interpretation. AO2
6. The topic sentence here establishes the focus of the paragraph. AO1
7. The alternative interpretation is well discussed and added in with care. AO2
8. The textual evidence is well embedded and relevant. AO1
9. Use of subject terminology is accurate and focused on effect. AO2
10. The writer's intention is discussed in relation to the question. AO3

Questions

EXAM PRACTICE
Spend 45 minutes writing an answer to the following question:
Explore how Sylvia is contrasted with her sister Maureen.
Write about:
- how Sylvia's character is different from Maureen's
- how Sylvia treats Leon differently from Maureen.   (30 marks + 4 AO4 marks)

The Exam

Planning a Theme Question Response

You must be able to: understand what an exam question is asking you and prepare your response.

How might an exam question on theme be phrased?

A typical theme question will usually look like this:

> Explore how *My Name is Leon* deals with the theme of growing up.
>
> Write about:
> - the way De Waal presents aspects of Leon's childhood
> - the way De Waal focuses on growing up.   (30 marks + 4 AO4 marks)

How do I work out what to do?

Work out the focus of the question – the bullet points will offer useful guidance. The main theme is childhood and how that is presented throughout the novel.

'How' is an important key word. For AO1, you need to show an understanding of how De Waal uses Leon as a character to show the challenges of growing up with an unstable home life. For AO2, the word 'how' means you need to analyse the way De Waal uses language, structure and form to shape the reader's understanding of childhood. While it is good to have quoted evidence, you can also use clear references to specific parts of the novel.

You also need to remember to link your answer to context to achieve the AO3 marks, and to write accurately to gain the full AO4 marks for spelling, punctuation and grammar.

How can I plan my essay?

You have 45 minutes to answer this question. This isn't long but you should spend the first five to ten minutes writing a quick plan. This will help you to focus your thoughts and produce a well-structured essay, which is an essential part of AO1. You should then spend 30–35 minutes writing, leaving yourself around five minutes for checking your answer.

Try to think of five or six ideas; each of these can become a paragraph. If possible, add a quick reminder of a quote or context you could write about, but focus on getting the main paragraph ideas down.

You can plan in whatever way you find most useful. Some students like to just make a quick list of points and then re-number them into a logical order or to create a flowchart. Spider diagrams are particularly popular; look at the example on the next page.

Childhood and growing up

- Leon is often presented as looking 'big for his age', which is mentioned from the very beginning of the novel. As a result of his mature appearance, he is often treated differently.
- Carol's immaturity is highlighted through the text. Her helplessness means that Leon is often forced to behave in an adult manner.
- Maureen's maternal nature juxtaposes with Carol's ineptitude.
- De Waal uses the motif of plants growing to represent how Leon should have been nurtured.
- The novel is told through a third-person perspective but has Leon as the focaliser.

Summary

- Make sure you understand the focus of the question (AO1).
- Analyse how the writer conveys ideas through the use of language, structure and form (AO2).
- Link ideas to social and historical context (AO3).
- Ensure your writing is clear and that you use accurate spelling, punctuation and grammar (AO4).

Questions

QUICK TEST
1. What key skills do you need to include in your answers?
2. What timing should you use?
3. Why is planning important?

EXAM PRACTICE
Plan the following question:
How does De Waal present the theme of racism throughout the text?
Write about:
- how race is presented
- how the effects of racial discrimination are presented.   (30 marks + 4 AO4 marks)

Planning a Theme Question Response

The Exam
Grade 5 Annotated Response

Explore how *My Name is Leon* explores the theme of growing up.
Write about:
- the way De Waal presents aspects of Leon's childhood
- the way De Waal focuses on growing up. (30 marks + 4 AO4 marks)

Throughout the novel 'My Name is Leon', Kit de Waal presents the theme of growing up through the character of Leon. (1) By having the main character be a child, De Waal ensures that we grow with the character.

(2) At the beginning of the novel, De Waal presents Leon as innocent and loving. The beginning of the novel coincides with the birth of Jake. It's almost as if the birth of Jake is a new beginning in Leon's life. However, rather than it being purely a happy occasion, Leon's mother's mental health soon becomes challenging and she loses all control. Chapter 3 begins with Leon noticing 'the things that make his mum cry'. (3) By opening the chapter in this way, De Waal is hinting at the more challenging problems that lay ahead. The simplistic language creates a very childish perspective, emphasising Leon's youth. (4)

A key feature of Leon's childhood is that he is often described as being 'big for his age'. (5) In fact, a nurse in Chapter 1 calls him a 'right little man'. While this is seen as a compliment, it becomes obvious that Leon is a child trapped in a teenager's body. (6)

(7) As Leon gets older, De Waal employs the use of seeds to represent Leon maturing and blossoming into a young man. (8) In Chapter 20, Tufty describes the seeds as 'babies' and 'fragile'. This becomes a metaphor for Leon because, just like the seeds, he needs to be looked after. (9)

To conclude, throughout the text, Leon faces many challenges that exceed his young age. (10)

1. The response begins by focusing on Leon. AO1
2. Topic sentence is clear and well written. AO1/AO4
3. Use of quotation is relevant to the paragraph. AO1
4. Some good analysis here with an understanding of how the writer uses language to create meaning. AO2
5. Topic sentence and evidence are both written with clarity. AO1
6. Analysis of language considers more than one perspective. AO2
7. Good use of discourse marker to open a new paragraph. AO1 AO4
8. The topic sentence also mentions the writer's intention. AO1 AO3
9. The discussion of the writer's methods is thoughtful and clear. AO2
10. A clear ending that summarises the argument of the essay. AO1

Questions

EXAM PRACTICE
Choose a paragraph of this essay. Read it through a few times and then try to improve it. You might:
- change or edit the quotations used to improve relevance
- analyse a quotation with more detail
- improve the range of analysis – go deeper with different ideas
- improve expression with more sophisticated vocabulary
- connect more analysis to the paragraph.

The Exam: Grade 7+ Annotated Response

Explore how *My Name is Leon* explores the theme of growing up.

Write about:
- the way De Waal presents aspects of Leon's childhood
- the way De Waal focuses on growing up.

(30 marks + 4 AO4 marks)

The themes of childhood and growing up are fundamental to understanding De Waal's novel. (1) De Waal presents the challenges of the social care system through the perspective of a young boy whose childhood has been interrupted due to the ignorance and the immaturity of those around him. (2)

When we are first introduced to Leon, a key feature is his appearance. In Chapter 1, a nurse says, 'you're nice and big for your age. A right little man.' Ostensibly this is presented as a compliment, suggesting Leon's maturity, both physically and emotionally. However, the emphasis on him being a 'man' foreshadows the stripping away of his childhood that becomes prominent as the novel develops. (3) Interestingly, the juxtaposition of 'little' and 'man' seems almost contradictory, however this becomes almost emblematic of the precarious position that Leon finds himself in throughout the novel. He is still 'little', a child in the eyes of the law, but he has to begin to think and act as close to an adult as he can, due to the maltreatment he suffers. (4)

While Leon is presented as mature, Carol, his mother, is significantly less so. At times, De Waal seems to be emphasising Carol's vulnerability. For instance, it is mentioned in Chapter 5 that Leon 'has to look after Jake nearly every day' while 'Carol keeps crying and going to the phone box'. Here, the role of mother and child are almost subverted. (5) Carol's helpless state of crying is reminiscent of a child, whereas Leon is left with the burden of responsibility of being his baby brother's caregiver. It is interesting to note that, at this point and many other points, Leon calls his mother by her first name. Once again, this exacerbates the slightly detached approach to parenting that Carol has. De Waal could be suggesting that Carol is desperately trying to disassociate herself from her maternal responsibilities. (6)

(7) A key motif that is used throughout the text is that of horticultural imagery, specifically seeds, which become metaphorical of Leon growing up. Tufty, who becomes a pseudo-paternal figure for him, states that the seeds are 'babies' and that they are 'fragile' and 'need looking after'. Each of these terms could also be used to describe Leon himself; he too is fragile, but his fragility is often ignored due to the preconception of his maturity. (8) However, his fragility is at the core of the novel, showing us the damaging results of a care system that is woefully

underfunded. The notion that babies need 'looking after' is something that Leon deeply understands in relation to his brother Jake. However, what Leon does not seem to understand is that he too is a child in need of care. This evokes an immense pathos as it reveals that, despite Leon's relative maturity, he still does not understand the lack of nurture he has been given. (9)

In conclusion, the character of Leon becomes a microcosm for De Waal to explore the challenges of life in the care system. De Waal herself grew up in a household where young people were fostered by her mother, so perhaps the choice to use the bildungsroman is a means of her giving a voice to the voiceless. (10)

1. Clear opening that instantly answers the question. AO1
2. Thesis is developed further to give an overview of the text and how the theme is presented throughout. AO1
3. Mentioning foreshadowing shows an understanding of the text as a whole. AO1/AO2
4. Analysis is specific and layered. AO2
5. The use of tentative language helps to extend the analysis. AO2
6. The analysis here is very perceptive, helping to consider the writer's choices in a nuanced manner. Also, good use of vocabulary. AO2/AO4
7. The paragraph has a clear focus. AO1
8. Analysis is more developed here: it goes further to think about the depth of the analysis. AO2
9. A very personal response is added here. AO1
10. Use of context is woven in to build and complete the response. AO3

Questions

EXAM PRACTICE

Spend 45 minutes writing an answer to the following question:

Explore how the theme of family is presented in the novel.

Write about:
- how the writer presents Leon's experience of family
- how the writer uses relationships to explore the idea of family.

(30 marks + 4 AO4 marks)

Glossary

Adoption – Permanently taking another child into your family and raising them as if they were your own child.

Adultification – Treating a child like they are an adult, particularly by making them take on adult responsibilities. Another form of adultification comes when authority figures punish children for crimes or misdeeds as if they were adults. This has, historically, been more likely to happen to Black children.

Allotment – A small area of land in a communally held area which can be allocated to individuals to grow vegetables or flowers.

Autonomy – Having control over your life and what happens to you.

Bildungsroman – A genre of literature about a child who faces challenges as they grow up.

Caricature – A depiction of a person in which certain characteristics are simplified or exaggerated to create a comic or grotesque effect.

Diatribe – A forceful and angry speech or article which attacks someone or something.

Dichotomy – The division of something into two opposing parts, which often creates conflict or tension in a story.

Disparity – A lack of equality; often used to describe a social or economic condition that's considered unfairly unequal.

Dramatic foil – A character whose traits contrast with another character's to highlight or emphasise the other character's qualities.

Dramatic irony – When the full significance of a character's words or actions is clear to the audience or reader but not to the characters.

Empathy – The ability to understand another's feelings.

Epistolary text – A text that reads like a letter. In Chapter 12, De Waal interrupts the third-person narration of the novel with a letter from Social Services.

Foreshadowing – Hinting at something that is going to happen later.

Foster parent – Someone who looks after a child who cannot live with their biological parents. This is not usually a permanent arrangement.

Hierarchy – A system that organises or ranks things, usually based on power or importance.

Idiosyncratic – Having habits or features that could be considered unique or unusual.

Infantilisation – Treating an adult like they are a child.

Juxtaposition – Placing two things next to each other, usually to create a contrast.

Malnourished – When someone's diet doesn't provide enough calories or nutrients.

Manipulative – To influence someone or something to your benefit in a clever and often selfish way.

Metaphor – A descriptive technique, using comparison to say one thing is something else.

Multiculturalism – When people from different cultures and backgrounds live alongside each other; interacting within one society.

Naïve – Showing a lack of experience and being too ready to believe someone or something.

Nurturer – Someone who takes care of someone, encourages them and provides for their needs.

Ominous – A sense of foreboding, a feeling that something bad is going to happen.

Protagonist – The main character of a novel – usually the one the reader principally identifies with. Leon is the protagonist of this text.

Simile – A descriptive technique that uses like or as to form a comparison.

Social Services – A range of public services designed to protect the wellbeing of children and vulnerable adults.

Social worker – A trained professional employed by Social Services to help people who need care, especially children.

Stigma – A set of negative and often unfair beliefs that society holds towards certain people. People can be stigmatised for their ethnicity, gender, life circumstances, upbringing and many other characteristics.

Stupor – An unresponsive state in which someone can't think or act normally.

Subtext – An implicit meaning that isn't clearly stated but is understood by the audience.

Third-person limited – A narrative viewpoint using the third person but focusing on the experience and perspective of one main character.

Visceral – Feelings that are intense, deep and often based on intuition rather than logical thought.

Answers

Pages 4–5
QUICK TEST
1. Leon is eight years old.
2. They think he is older than his age.
3. 1980
4. *The Dukes of Hazzard*
5. Tina

EXAM PRACTICE
Leon is seen to be instantly loving and caring towards his baby brother, naïvely telling him the things he thinks Jake needs to know, like what is the best TV programme. Leon looks old for eight, with the nurse calling him 'A right little man.' He has spent a lot of time with the neighbour, Tina, and her toddler Bobby loves him. Leon is responsible, as shown by his insistence that he 'won't drop' Jake.

Pages 6–7
QUICK TEST
1. She says the weather is too bad for him to go.
2. 'What about his daughter?'
3. That he is observant and very much tuned in to his mother.
4. That he will look after Jake and himself.
5. So he can train it to bite Jake's father and other people who annoy him.

EXAM PRACTICE
Carol often falls short of meeting her parental obligations and relies heavily upon Leon's responsible attitude and willingness to look after Jake (e.g. keeping him off school on the pretext that it is 'too wet and rainy'). She looks tired and it is becoming apparent that she can't cope with her own emotions, which impacts her ability to care for her children. Lots of things make Carol cry, hinting at her poor mental health. She is also a fantasist (e.g. being convinced that Jake's father will leave his partner for her) and when this does not happen it further affects her mental health.

Pages 8–9
QUICK TEST
1. Some coins
2. Carol was relying heavily on Tina for childcare and borrowing money from her.
3. It was partly based on both of them being heavy drinkers.
4. A Jammie Dodger biscuit
5. Kids

EXAM PRACTICE
Carol cannot keep Leon fed, while Maureen feeds him extremely well. When Carol becomes ill, Leon can go to bed whenever he wants and eat whatever he wants, but there is no food to eat. Maureen, on the other hand, starts feeding him as soon as he arrives and sets boundaries (e.g., bedtimes). When Maureen makes him a sandwich, 'It tastes like the best thing in the world'. Similarly, when Jake 'has been crying all morning … Carol won't do anything', whereas Maureen asks Leon what Jake's routine and looks after both children.

Pages 10–11
QUICK TEST
1. He is frustrated at being treated like a child.
2. Action Man dolls
3. He's a baby and he's white.
4. She asks if he loves Jake.
5. He is sad and angry.

EXAM PRACTICE
Maureen is almost brutally honest with Leon about why Jake is being adopted – because he's 'a white baby'. When Jake's adoptive parents arrive, they show no interest in Leon: 'The lady doesn't look at Leon, she only looks at Jake …'. The effect of their racial difference is to split them up, because Social Services have decided it is better to have just Jake adopted than neither of them. There is a suggestion that Jake's best interests are prioritised over Leon's.

Pages 12–13
QUICK TEST
1. Grinding his teeth
2. A Social Services report
3. She is having a mental health crisis.
4. Detached/professional
5. To see a doctor

EXAM PRACTICE
Leon is woken by nightmares, such as one in which he is 'fighting an evil monster', which seems to show his sense of threat and insecurity. He also grinds his teeth in his sleep, another sign of anxiety. He has moved on from stealing to vandalising Salma's bag, making a 'brown sticky mess' in it. This seems to be the only way he can feel any sense of autonomy in the wake of losing both his mother and his brother and having to leave his old home, along with most of his toys.

Pages 14–15
QUICK TEST
1. She collapses to the floor.
2. The photo of Jake
3. A pencil and pen set in a wooden box
4. Sylvia
5. A BMX bike

EXAM PRACTICE
One of the ways De Waal uses Carol and Maureen as dramatic foils to each other is in relation to the gifts they give Leon. When Carol comes to visit Leon, she gives him a pencil and pen set in a wooden box – which, as his mother, she ought to know is not the kind of present he would appreciate. This could be compared with the thoughtfully chosen Christmas presents Maureen gives him – an Action Man and a *Dukes of Hazzard* racing set. She has taken note of what he really likes. In addition, when Carol visits Leon, she focuses more on having lost Jake than on seeing Leon. She has to be reminded by Maureen that it is hard for Leon too. While Carol becomes increasingly unreliable, Maureen is a consistent loving presence in his life.

Pages 16–17
QUICK TEST
1. Star
2. A cream soda
3. The Zebra
4. His Japanese knife
5. Racism and police brutality

EXAM PRACTICE
Tufty is friendly towards Leon, giving him a cream soda as soon as he meets him and giving him the positive nickname 'Star'. His friendliness is shown by his 'wide smile'. He shows Leon how to plant and care for seeds, becoming a parental figure to him. When Tufty talks about seeds, it could also be a metaphor for Leon: '… babies. Fragile. Babies need looking after.' This offers a stark contrast to the adultification of Leon by many characters throughout the text. Tufty also introduces Leon to Black cultural figures, helping to give him a sense of identity and a pride in what he has inherited from his own father, Byron.

Pages 18–19
QUICK TEST
1. Switch off the people he doesn't like
2. Tufty
3. The Zebra
4. She is much thinner, looks depressed and plays with a doll.
5. Jake

EXAM PRACTICE
De Waal uses contrasting historical events to provide context to Leon's experiences. On the one hand, the reader sees Sylvia and her friend enthusiastically planning a community street party to celebrate the Royal Wedding. This seems to be a positive coming together of the nation – or at least of those who identify with the Royal Family. A different kind of 'community event' is shown in the rioting that appears on the news, making Sylvia jump up in alarm when a nearby street is mentioned. The rioting shows unrest that is reflected in Leon's personal unrest. Ironically, Sylvia's distraction provides him with another opportunity to steal from her purse.

Pages 20–21
QUICK TEST
1. She tells him funny stories.
2. Mr Devlin
3. He reveals a gentler side.
4. Castro
5. Arrest him for stealing

EXAM PRACTICE
Leon's nightmare in which he is in a cooking pot and about to be eaten by an ogre seems to represent the sense of threat and insecurity he feels because of his displacement, the loss of his mother and brother and his dislike of school. It may even relate to his fears that he will eventually be caught and punished for his stealing – though he carries on doing it because it gives him a sense of power. The objects Leon sees and is fascinated by in Mr Devlin's shed, including knives and what appears to be a gun, could also symbolise his insecurity in that they feed into his fantasies of self-defence.

Pages 22–23
QUICK TEST
1. Mike/Earring
2. Mr Devlin
3. He knows that Jake's new parents wrote it.
4. The pistol
5. His mother, Carol

EXAM PRACTICE
Sadly, part of Leon's growing up is shown in his becoming increasingly disillusioned, even cynical. When a new social worker visits, 'Leon knows every word that he's going to say' because he's heard it all before. Another aspect of his growing up is his witnessing his hero Tufty having a violent row with Mr Devlin, who is also a paternal figure to Leon in a more detached way. When Mr Devlin arranges for Leon to have a small allotment, his own 'small patch of the planet', this is significant because it represents something for which Leon will have to take responsibility. In a sense, he is taking charge of his own growth.

Pages 24–25
QUICK TEST
1. Brazil
2. Castro
3. Jars of baby food
4. 'Ode to Castro'
5. The seaside

EXAM PRACTICE
Tufty shows his desire to protect Leon in a fatherly way when he asks, referring to Mr Devlin, 'He touch you?' In fact, Tufty has the wrong idea about Mr Devlin, but at least he cares. His protection is better directed when he saves Leon from the desperate Castro, who is hiding from the police in Tufty's shed. Tufty's paternal role is made clearer in the line 'Sometimes, when Tufty is talking, Leon thinks about his dad' reinforcing the importance of Tufty's positive impact on Leon's developing understanding of his own identity. Tufty also influences Leon by making him aware of Black heroes and through his poetry in which he states, 'We have dignity and worth.'

Pages 26–27
QUICK TEST
1. She uses a Greek Chorus approach and has Tufty report Castro's death rather than describing it directly.
2. To take with him when he goes to Bristol to find Jake.
3. 'savages'
4. He has been killed by the police.
5. Bristol, to see Jake

EXAM PRACTICE
Tension increases during these chapters due to a number of factors. First, there is Leon's secret plan to escape from Sylvia's house, find Jake and take him to Bristol to reunite with Carol. The reader can guess that in a realistic book like this, the plan is very unlikely to succeed. Both his level of planning and his naïve inability to carry out the plan are shown in the undifferentiated list of things he has acquired to help him, including Mr Devlin's 'gun'. At the social level, the police brutality glimpsed earlier in the novel now comes to a head in Castro's murder, which leads to rioting just as Leon is attempting his escape plan. The tension is ramped up at the allotments, with Tufty and Mr Devlin arguing and then both searching in the dark for Leon.

Pages 28–29
QUICK TEST
1. Mr Devlin
2. Tufty
3. She says he will continue to live with her.
4. The Royal Wedding
5. Mr Devlin

EXAM PRACTICE
By the end of the novel, the two father figures in Leon's life, Tufty and Mr Devlin, seem to have overcome their mutual dislike and animosity through having to help each other during the riot. In addition, Mr Devlin is romantically involved with Sylvia. Leon has promised Maureen to be open with her and not to run away again. Maureen is out of hospital and living with Sylvia, and has established that Leon can stay with her for good. On the other hand, Leon may never see Jake again and his mother has told him, 'I can't look after you properly'. Leon has an extended family, comprised of adults who are invested in supporting and nurturing him. Although it is not the arrangement that he had originally wanted or fantasised about, it is safe and secure.

Pages 30–31
QUICK TEST
1. Third-person limited
2. Leon reads a letter from Social Services about his mother.
3. Leon's eavesdropping is used to reveal other characters' thoughts.
4. Mr Devlin

EXAM PRACTICE
De Waal's use of a third-person limited narrative perspective builds empathy for Leon, because the entire story is told from his viewpoint. This means that the reader is often given Leon's perception of events without any interpretation or analysis. An example is in the opening to Chapter 3, 'Leon has begun to notice the things that make his mum cry'. This shows that he is observant and sympathetic, but it lacks the adult overview that would conclude that she is bordering on a breakdown. He becomes adept at 'reading' the emotions of others, as shown in 'He can tell when Maureen's trying to be happy and when she's worried'. Again, this shows his observation and sensitivity, and builds empathy because his reading of others seems necessary to his own survival.

Pages 32–33
QUICK TEST
1. Handsworth, Birmingham
2. 1981
3. Chaos
4. Food-related imagery
5. They represent Leon's growth as a character.

EXAM PRACTICE
Leon's emotional state is often shown through setting. For example, in Carol's house, as her mental health declines, his physical and emotional deprivation are shown through there being 'nothing in the fridge and nothing in the cupboard'. By contrast, at Maureen's, 'Leon is in a soft, warm bed and there are black-and-white footballs on his quilt'. Here, the bed represents security. Sylvia also provides him with physical comfort, but with less understanding of what a boy his age might like: 'The sheets on his new bed in Sylvia's house. They're pink.'

Pages 34–35
QUICK TEST
1. Leon might reflect both De Waal's own knowledge of the care system as well as her mother's experiences as a carer.
2. That it often neglects those it is supposed to care for, but that there are also social workers and foster carers who do their best to connect with the children in their care.
3. The race riots in Handsworth are portrayed unflinchingly.
4. Margaret Thatcher
5. The Royal Wedding

EXAM PRACTICE
Nothing can excuse the police officer's racism and threat of violence, but they can be seen in the context of Leon, like a lot of Black boys, being perceived as a lot older than he is. De Waal captures the longstanding narrative to justify police brutality towards Black boys. De Waal's description of 'fires burning in the streets and clashes between police and gangs of youths' references the social unrest of the time, especially the riots in Brixton and in Handsworth where the novel is set. When Tufty asks Mr Devlin if he finds it 'funny that the police kill black people?', he is misjudging Mr Devlin, but his sensitivity is understandable in the context of the racism of the period.

Pages 36–37
QUICK TEST
1. To focus the reader's attention on social issues
2. The working and lower classes
3. The Handsworth Riots /IRA hunger strikes/police brutality
4. Charles Dickens
5. The prevalence of racism

Exam Question
The novel is in many ways an example of literary realism, showing life like it is. Maureen, for example, tells Leon the simple truth about why Jake is being adopted and not him: 'Because he's a baby, a white baby. And you're not.' Her honest statement reveals the racism of the time. The novel also deals with social unrest, especially among people living as minorities in the UK: 'the riots and the Irishman that starved himself to death'. This is literary realism as it examines difficult social issues and the suffering they cause. De Waal's approach is interesting as it often shows hard social truths through Leon's naïve and simple observations, as in 'I saw some policemen today and they were fighting with two black men'. This leaves the reader to reach their own conclusions.

Pages 38–39

1. That he is intelligent, observant and responsible.
2. He steals
3. His adoration of Jake
4. Tufty
5. Her sense of humour

EXAM PRACTICE
Leon's most endearing and enduring characteristic is his love for his baby brother. The reader sees this when he patiently introduces himself to Jake in Chapter 1: 'My. Name. Is. Leon.' He works hard, and willingly, to look after Jake and then Carol as she becomes more ill. A less appealing feature is his stealing, which seems to be his way of claiming some level of autonomy when so much has been taken from him. He even steals from people who have cared for him. His occasional lies, such as when he tells Sylvia that his 'mum and dad have a massive garden' can be seen as a childish wish-fulfilment fantasy.

Pages 40–41
QUICK TEST

1. She lets him call her by her first name.
2. His only photo of baby Jake
3. She becomes much thinner and less healthy and attractive.
4. That she can't look after him.
5. Her lack of reliability and constancy in Leon's life

EXAM PRACTICE
Carol is presented as negligent even in Chapter 1 when she puts off feeding her newborn baby to go and have a cigarette. Later she fails to feed Leon and relies on him to care for the baby. Even when she visits him at Maureen's house, she focuses more on having lost Jake than on being present for Leon, asking, 'Can I have that photo of my baby?' even though it is the only reminder of Jake that Leon has. It does not seem to occur to her that Leon misses Jake too. Her admission to Leon that 'I can't look after you properly' is a significant moment in the text, offering Leon some much-needed closure.

Pages 42–43
QUICK TEST

1. A photograph of Jake
2. De Waal's own mother
3. Children
4. Tightness in her chest
5. It means the reader misses her, as Leon does.

EXAM PRACTICE
Carol fails to feed Leon, both physically and emotionally, as shown by her empty fridge and cupboard, whereas Maureen is always feeding him and he can't decide which of her meals is his favourite. She is confident of her knowledge of children, saying she has 'an eye for kids', and expresses her love and care for Leon very clearly: 'I think about you and I care for you and I love you'. Carol, on the other hand, does love him in her own way, but has to admit that she can't look after him 'properly'.

Pages 44–45
QUICK TEST

1. Maureen is unable to look after him when she is in hospital.
2. She speaks about her and Maureen's future without including Leon.
3. She tells him funny stories.
4. They both involve someone being cruel to someone gullible.
5. Mr Devlin

EXAM PRACTICE
Leon does not immediately take to Sylvia and when he makes a list of things he does not like, it begins with her and mostly contains things that relate to her. This is not surprising as he has lost his mother and brother and bonded with Maureen and now has to adjust to yet another carer. However, she is good to him in her own way. Even when Leon loses his temper and deliberately makes a mess of the bathroom, she responds fairly and calmly, simply showing him that he cannot get away with that behaviour, even if he is upset. A key positive feature of her character is her rather dark sense of humour, seen when she offers to bring him a picnic to share with his (non-existent) friends and then says, 'Bet you'd rather have your nails dipped in acid'. Her joke shows that she is aware that bringing him a picnic would embarrass him. At the end of the novel, we see a softer side to her character when she is apparently in a relationship with Mr Devlin and Maureen says, 'He's got you like a sixteen-year-old'. This shows her more vulnerable side, and that even she can overcome her disillusionment.

Pages 46–47
QUICK TEST

1. Reggae and Dub, Black-led music genres
2. A cream soda
3. Racial injustice
4. Pictures of Black heroes
5. He thinks Mr Devlin was responsible for him losing his allotment, and also that he is a paedophile.

EXAM PRACTICE
Tufty is an important character because he is immediately kind and friendly to Leon, offering him a cream soda and calling him 'Star'. He introduces Leon to gardening, teaching him to plant seeds – which is also a metaphor for Leon himself. He protects Leon from Castro, wants to protect him from Mr Devlin and introduces him to kung fu and Black music, politics and culture. He sets Leon a good example, as a man who is kind and reliable, assertive but not violent. His 'Ode to Castro' asserts: 'I don't want to be a warrior / I didn't come for war'. He is prepared to stand up to police racism, as when he protests, 'Leave him! Leave him! He can't breathe', but he is not antagonistic.

Pages 48–49
QUICK TEST

1. Cycling in the allotments
2. Photos of children and a gun
3. He misses his family in Brazil and his son.
4. His students in Brazil
5. Sylvia

EXAM PRACTICE
It could be argued that Mr Devlin is as important as Tufty, even though he is not immediately so appealing. He initially comes across as someone who is very keen on enforcing rules, telling Tufty off for cycling in the allotments; according to Tufty, he is 'So busy spying, he forgets to live his life'. Mr Devlin adds an important element of mystery and suspense. In addition to being another father figure to Leon, he also teaches both Leon and the reader that people may not be what they seem at first. His 'photographs of boys' have an entirely innocent explanation: he ran a school in Brazil. Moreover, the reader learns that there has been tragedy in his life and he now misses the school and his family: 'I was loved. They loved me'. This makes him a much more sympathetic character.

Pages 50–51
QUICK TEST

1. The Zebra
2. Brazil
3. Her deteriorating mental health
4. It is a focal point that brings people together.
5. The riot

EXAM PRACTICE
Carol gradually alienates Tina because she is always getting her to look after Leon and borrowing money and not repaying it. By the time of her overdose, when she responds to attempts to wake her with 'Leave me alone! Leave me alone!', she seems to find any demands on her too much to cope with, which increases her isolation. Leon suffers from her neglect and takes a lot of time off school to look after Jake and then his mother. She 'keeps crying and going to the phone box, leaving Leon in charge' because she is trying to speak to Jake's father, convinced that she can only be happy if he moves in with her. Leon becomes further isolated because he cannot admit to anyone what is happening at home. Even when he is living with Maureen, then Sylvia, he hates school and has no friends. Sylvia tells him, 'You should have friends, Leon', but she cannot make them for him.

Pages 52–53
QUICK TEST

1. Pictures of his Black heroes
2. 'Coloured'
3. He is a baby and he is white.
4. A policeman
5. The racism faced by Black people in the UK in the 1980s

EXAM PRACTICE
Leon feels different from both his parents as Carol is white and his father is Black: 'he's dark brown and I'm light brown'. However, the effects of his skin colour only really hit home when Maureen tells him the reason he is not being adopted: 'Because he's a baby, a white baby. And you're not'. In addition, as a mixed-race boy who looks much older than his actual age, he is sometimes treated like

a teenager. This is most obvious when a furious policeman comes close to clubbing him with his truncheon during the riot. Leon has done nothing to hurt or offend him, but the man 'screams' at him, 'You little black bastard!' The police officer sees only his colour and his size, and assumes that he is a threat, not a confused child.

Pages 54–55
QUICK TEST
1. They are both absent fathers.
2. He appears only in Leon's memories.
3. Maureen
4. They have both lost their mothers.
5. Brazil

EXAM PRACTICE
Before the start of the novel, Leon lives with both his parents, though the family seems dysfunctional, with both parents drinking and arguing. His father leaves before the book starts and he then loses his mother because the decline in her mental health means she is unable to care for him. Then Jake is adopted, with a social worker trying to convince Leon that it would be good for 'Jake to be in a family with a mum and dad of his own' even though this will mean that Leon never sees him again. However, Maureen, a woman with 'an eye for children', and who tells him she loves him, becomes his foster parent, taking on the maternal role. Leon's father, who thinks he has 'no one now' when his own mother dies, is absent, but the paternal role is taken by Tufty and Mr Devlin. Leon's new 'family' is cemented by the two men overcoming their differences: 'Leon likes it when they pretend to argue like they used to'. Leon now has a less conventional but more supportive family than he originally had.

Pages 56–57
Quick Questions
1. He looks after his mother and his brother.
2. Action Man dolls
3. As a brave soldier
4. James Bond
5. He has been in care before.

EXAM PRACTICE
Leon looks older than he is, but he is still very much a child. He loves to play with his Action Man dolls and assumes that when Jake is older, 'they're going to play together, soldiers and Action Man'. As a naïve child, it does not occur to him that by the time Jake can do this, he (Leon) will no longer want to play the same games. He has childish fantasies, picturing himself as a soldier 'creeping through the jungle with his men'. Ironically, he actually wants to look older than he is, thinking that 'with his new bike, he could even be fourteen', little realising the danger this could put him in because of the way in which the police may regard him.

Pages 58–59
QUICK TEST
1. She is crying frequently.
2. He says it is like a rusty motor.
3. He has bad dreams, steals and struggles with anger.
4. In a letter that drops out of a Social Services file
5. A BMX bike

EXAM PRACTICE
Leon is in some ways mature and is happy to take responsibility for his brother and even his mother when she 'keeps crying and going to the phone box' to plead with Jake's father to leave his partner for her. She is deluded in thinking he will do this, and Leon is a victim of Carol's mental ill health. This leads to him being at the mercy of an impersonal Social Services system, represented by 'Earring', whom Leon finds depressingly predictable: 'Leon knows every word that he's going to say'. Leon's own mental health suffers too, as shown by his nightmares, his stealing and his angry, violent fantasies, such as stabbing Earring in the eye with his own pen. Carol's mental health declines, as eventually shown by her playing with a doll, but she finally recognises and admits that she cannot look after Leon.

Pages 64–65, 68–69, 70–71 and 74–75
QUICK TEST
1. Answer the question directly; include and analyse relevant quotations; include and analyse the relevance of historical context.
2. 5–10 minutes planning, 30–35 minutes writing, 5 minutes checking your answer.
3. It allows you to write a well-structured essay with all of the key skills clearly demonstrated. This is very hard to do if you are making up your essay as you go along.

Exam Practice – Character (1)
Answers might explore: Carol is loving at first, saying she has 'two beautiful boys', though she already shows signs of neglecting her parental duties when she prioritises smoking a cigarette before feeding Jake; she relies more and more on Leon's willingness to care for Jake; her blaming him for making Tony leave; her drug dependency; the way she focuses more on her loss of Jake when she finally visits Leon; her becoming childlike; and her admitting that she cannot look after him 'properly'.

Exam Practice – Character (2)
Answers might explore: the fact that Sylvia is not a mother and has not fostered children; her 'tough love' approach, including laying down boundaries for Leon and making him clear up the mess he makes when Earring has upset him; Sylvia's quirky sense of humour; the fact that Maureen is more conventionally maternal, though Sylvia cares for Leon in her own way.

Exam Practice – Themes (1)
Answers might explore: the reasons for Leon not being adopted; Tufty's attitude towards the police harassment of Castro, and of Black people generally; the police visit to the allotments; the police murder of Castro and the policeman's treatment of Leon during the riots; the racially influenced attitudes that Tufty and Devlin have towards each other.

Exam Practice – Themes (2)
Answers might explore: Leon's initial lack of a two-parent family and how it contrasts with the unconventional family he has at the end of the novel; how Carol fails to cope as a single parent; how Leon himself tries to make up for Carol's inadequacies; how Tufty and Mr Devlin become father figures to Leon; how Leon's new family is cemented by his living with Maureen and Sylvia, and by Sylvia forming a relationship with Mr Devlin.

Pages 68–69 and 74–75
EXAM PRACTICE
Use the mark scheme below to self-assess your strengths and weaknesses. Work up from the bottom, putting a tick by things you have fully accomplished, a ½ by skills that are in place but need securing and underlining areas that need particular development. The estimated grade boundaries are included so you can assess your progress towards your target grade.

Grade	AO1 (12 marks)	AO2 (12 marks)	AO3 (6 marks)
6–7+	A convincing, well-structured essay that answers the question fully. Quotations and references are well-chosen and integrated into sentences. The response covers the whole novel.	Analysis of the full range of De Waal's methods. Thorough exploration of the effects of these methods. Accurate range of subject terminology.	Exploration is linked to specific aspects of the novel's contexts to show a detailed understanding.
4–5	A clear essay that always focuses on the exam question. Quotations and references support ideas effectively. The response refers to different points in the novel.	Explanation of De Waal's different methods. Clear understanding of the effects of these methods. Accurate use of subject terminology.	References to relevant aspects of context show a clear understanding.
2–3	The essay has some good ideas that are mostly relevant. Some quotations and references are used to support the ideas.	Identification of some different methods used by De Waal to convey meaning. Some subject terminology.	Some awareness of how ideas in the novel link to its context.